THIS BOOK BELONGS TO:

_____

_____

INDEX

Page	Tea	Page	Tea
1		27	
2		28	
3		29	
4		30	
5		31	
6		32	
7		33	
8		34	
9		35	
10		36	
11		37	
12		38	
13		39	
14		40	
15		41	
16		42	
17		43	
18		44	
19		45	
20		46	
21		47	
22		48	
23		49	
24		50	
25		51	
26		52	

INDEX

Page	Tea	Page	Tea
53		79	
54		80	
55		81	
56		82	
57		83	
58		84	
59		85	
60		86	
61		87	
62		88	
63		89	
64		90	
65		91	
66		92	
67		93	
68		94	
69		95	
70		96	
71		97	
72		98	
73		99	
74		100	
75		101	
76		102	
77		103	
78		104	

TEA Tasting

NAME	
ORIGIN	METHOD
VENDOR	MEASURE
PRICE	STEEP TIME
TASTING DATE	TEMP

🍵 TEA TYPE

☐ White ☐ Green ☐ Oolong ☐ Black ☐ Pu-erh ☐ Herbal ☐

🌿 DRY LEAF

🌱 INFUSED LEAF

☕ LIQUOR

LOOK

☐ Clear ☐ Semi-Cloudy ☐ Cloudy

_____
_____

AROMA

☐ Low ☐ Med. ☐ High Complexity

_____
_____
_____
_____
_____

PALATE

☐ Bright ☐ Smooth ☐ Light
☐ Soft ☐ Medium ☐ Medium
☐ Dull ☐ Harsh ☐ Full-Bodied

_____
_____
_____
_____
_____
_____

FINISH

☐ Short ☐ Medium ☐ Long

_____
_____
_____

😋 FLAVOR WHEEL

Earthy / Woodsy
Smoky
Nutty / Malty
Sweet
Metallic
Sour
Fruity
Milky
Spicy
Bitter
Herbal
Mineral
Vegetal
Muscatel
Grassy
Flowery

💬 ADDITIONAL NOTES

🧊 PREPARED WITH

☐ Milk ☐ Lemon
☐ Sugar ☐ Honey
☐ Cream ☐

☆ SCORE

/5 ☆

1

TEA Tasting

NAME	
ORIGIN	METHOD
VENDOR	MEASURE
PRICE	STEEP TIME
TASTING DATE	TEMP

🍵 TEA TYPE

☐ White ☐ Green ☐ Oolong ☐ Black ☐ Pu-erh ☐ Herbal ☐

🌿 DRY LEAF	🌿 INFUSED LEAF

☕ LIQUOR

👁 LOOK
☐ Clear ☐ Semi-Cloudy ☐ Cloudy
_____
_____

👃 AROMA
☐ Low ☐ Med. ☐ High Complexity
_____
_____
_____
_____

👅 PALATE
☐ Bright ☐ Smooth ☐ Light
☐ Soft ☐ Medium ☐ Medium
☐ Dull ☐ Harsh ☐ Full-Bodied
_____
_____
_____
_____
_____
_____

👄 FINISH
☐ Short ☐ Medium ☐ Long
_____
_____
_____

😋 FLAVOR WHEEL

Earthy / Woodsy • Smoky • Nutty / Malty
Sweet
Sour • Metallic
Fruity • Milky
Spicy • Bitter
Herbal • Mineral
Vegetal • Muscatel
Grassy • Flowery

💬 ADDITIONAL NOTES

_____
_____
_____
_____
_____
_____
_____
_____
_____
_____

🍶 PREPARED WITH

☐ Milk ☐ Lemon
☐ Sugar ☐ Honey
☐ Cream ☐

☆ SCORE

/5 ☆

TEA Tasting

NAME	
ORIGIN	METHOD
VENDOR	MEASURE
PRICE	STEEP TIME
TASTING DATE	TEMP

🔖 TEA TYPE

☐ White ☐ Green ☐ Oolong ☐ Black ☐ Pu-erh ☐ Herbal ☐

🌱 DRY LEAF

🌿 INFUSED LEAF

☕ LIQUOR

LOOK

☐ Clear ☐ Semi-Cloudy ☐ Cloudy

_____
_____

AROMA

☐ Low ☐ Med. ☐ High Complexity

_____
_____
_____
_____

PALATE

☐ Bright ☐ Smooth ☐ Light
☐ Soft ☐ Medium ☐ Medium
☐ Dull ☐ Harsh ☐ Full-Bodied

_____
_____
_____
_____
_____
_____
_____

FINISH

☐ Short ☐ Medium ☐ Long

_____
_____
_____

😋 FLAVOR WHEEL

Earthy / Woodsy, Smoky, Nutty / Malty, Sweet, Sour, Metallic, Fruity, Milky, Spicy, Bitter, Herbal, Mineral, Vegetal, Muscatel, Grassy, Flowery

💬 ADDITIONAL NOTES

_____
_____
_____
_____
_____
_____
_____
_____
_____
_____
_____

🍬 PREPARED WITH

☐ Milk ☐ Lemon
☐ Sugar ☐ Honey
☐ Cream ☐

⭐ SCORE

/5 ☆

3

TEA Tasting

NAME	
ORIGIN	METHOD
VENDOR	MEASURE
PRICE	STEEP TIME
TASTING DATE	TEMP

🏷 TEA TYPE

☐ White ☐ Green ☐ Oolong ☐ Black ☐ Pu-erh ☐ Herbal ☐

🌿 DRY LEAF

🌱 INFUSED LEAF

☕ LIQUOR

👁 LOOK
☐ Clear ☐ Semi-Cloudy ☐ Cloudy
_____
_____

👃 AROMA
☐ Low ☐ Med. ☐ High Complexity
_____
_____
_____
_____
_____

👅 PALATE
☐ Bright ☐ Smooth ☐ Light
☐ Soft ☐ Medium ☐ Medium
☐ Dull ☐ Harsh ☐ Full-Bodied
_____
_____
_____
_____
_____
_____
_____

👄 FINISH
☐ Short ☐ Medium ☐ Long
_____
_____
_____

😋 FLAVOR WHEEL

Earthy/Woodsy Smoky Nutty/Malty
Sweet Metallic
Sour
Fruity Milky
Spicy Bitter
Herbal Mineral
Vegetal Muscatel
Grassy Flowery

💬 ADDITIONAL NOTES

_____
_____
_____
_____
_____
_____
_____
_____
_____
_____
_____
_____

🧊 PREPARED WITH

☐ Milk ☐ Lemon
☐ Sugar ☐ Honey
☐ Cream ☐

⭐ SCORE

/5 ☆

TEA Tasting

NAME	
ORIGIN	METHOD
VENDOR	MEASURE
PRICE	STEEP TIME
TASTING DATE	TEMP

🏷️ TEA TYPE

☐ White ☐ Green ☐ Oolong ☐ Black ☐ Pu-erh ☐ Herbal ☐

🌿 DRY LEAF

🌱 INFUSED LEAF

☕ LIQUOR

LOOK 👁️
☐ Clear ☐ Semi-Cloudy ☐ Cloudy
_____
_____

AROMA 👃
☐ Low ☐ Med. ☐ High Complexity
_____
_____
_____
_____

PALATE 👅
☐ Bright ☐ Smooth ☐ Light
☐ Soft ☐ Medium ☐ Medium
☐ Dull ☐ Harsh ☐ Full-Bodied
_____
_____
_____
_____
_____
_____

FINISH 👄
☐ Short ☐ Medium ☐ Long
_____
_____
_____

😋 FLAVOR WHEEL

Earthy/Woodsy Smoky Nutty/Malty
Sweet Metallic
Sour
Fruity Milky
Spicy Bitter
Herbal Mineral
Vegetal Muscatel
Grassy Flowery

💬 ADDITIONAL NOTES

🧊 PREPARED WITH

☐ Milk ☐ Lemon
☐ Sugar ☐ Honey
☐ Cream ☐

☆ SCORE

/5 ☆

5

TEA
Tasting

NAME	
ORIGIN	METHOD
VENDOR	MEASURE
PRICE	STEEP TIME
TASTING DATE	TEMP

🔖 TEA TYPE

☐ White ☐ Green ☐ Oolong ☐ Black ☐ Pu-erh ☐ Herbal ☐

🌱 DRY LEAF

🌿 INFUSED LEAF

☕ LIQUOR

LOOK 👁

☐ Clear ☐ Semi-Cloudy ☐ Cloudy

_____
_____

AROMA 👃

☐ Low ☐ Med. ☐ High Complexity

_____
_____
_____
_____

PALATE 👅

☐ Bright ☐ Smooth ☐ Light
☐ Soft ☐ Medium ☐ Medium
☐ Dull ☐ Harsh ☐ Full-Bodied

_____
_____
_____
_____
_____
_____

FINISH 👄

☐ Short ☐ Medium ☐ Long

_____
_____
_____

😋 FLAVOR WHEEL

Earthy / Woodsy
Smoky
Nutty / Malty
Sweet
Sour
Metallic
Fruity
Milky
Spicy
Bitter
Herbal
Mineral
Vegetal
Muscatel
Grassy
Flowery

💬 ADDITIONAL NOTES

_____
_____
_____
_____
_____
_____
_____
_____
_____
_____

🧊 PREPARED WITH

☐ Milk ☐ Lemon
☐ Sugar ☐ Honey
☐ Cream ☐

☆ SCORE

/5 ☆

6

TEA Tasting

NAME	
ORIGIN	METHOD
VENDOR	MEASURE
PRICE	STEEP TIME
TASTING DATE	TEMP

🏷 TEA TYPE

☐ White ☐ Green ☐ Oolong ☐ Black ☐ Pu-erh ☐ Herbal ☐

🌿 DRY LEAF

🌱 INFUSED LEAF

☕ LIQUOR

👁 LOOK

☐ Clear ☐ Semi-Cloudy ☐ Cloudy
_____
_____

👃 AROMA

☐ Low ☐ Med. ☐ High Complexity
_____
_____
_____
_____
_____

👅 PALATE

☐ Bright ☐ Smooth ☐ Light
☐ Soft ☐ Medium ☐ Medium
☐ Dull ☐ Harsh ☐ Full-Bodied
_____
_____
_____
_____
_____
_____

👄 FINISH

☐ Short ☐ Medium ☐ Long
_____
_____
_____

😋 FLAVOR WHEEL

Earthy / Woodsy — Smoky — Nutty / Malty — Sweet — Sour — Metallic — Fruity — Milky — Spicy — Bitter — Herbal — Mineral — Vegetal — Muscatel — Grassy — Flowery

💬 ADDITIONAL NOTES

_____
_____
_____
_____
_____
_____
_____
_____
_____

🎲 PREPARED WITH

☐ Milk ☐ Lemon
☐ Sugar ☐ Honey
☐ Cream ☐

☆ SCORE

/5 ☆

7

TEA Tasting

NAME	
ORIGIN	METHOD
VENDOR	MEASURE
PRICE	STEEP TIME
TASTING DATE	TEMP

🫖 TEA TYPE

☐ White ☐ Green ☐ Oolong ☐ Black ☐ Pu-erh ☐ Herbal ☐

🌿 DRY LEAF	🌿 INFUSED LEAF

☕ LIQUOR

👁 LOOK
☐ Clear ☐ Semi-Cloudy ☐ Cloudy
_____
_____

👃 AROMA
☐ Low ☐ Med. ☐ High Complexity
_____
_____
_____
_____
_____

🫖 PALATE
☐ Bright ☐ Smooth ☐ Light
☐ Soft ☐ Medium ☐ Medium
☐ Dull ☐ Harsh ☐ Full-Bodied
_____
_____
_____
_____
_____
_____
_____

👄 FINISH
☐ Short ☐ Medium ☐ Long
_____
_____
_____

😊 FLAVOR WHEEL

Earthy / Woodsy, Smoky, Nutty / Malty, Sweet, Sour, Metallic, Fruity, Milky, Spicy, Bitter, Herbal, Mineral, Vegetal, Muscatel, Grassy, Flowery

💬 ADDITIONAL NOTES

_____
_____
_____
_____
_____
_____
_____
_____
_____
_____

🎲 PREPARED WITH

☐ Milk ☐ Lemon
☐ Sugar ☐ Honey
☐ Cream ☐

⭐ SCORE

/5 ☆

8

TEA Tasting

NAME	
ORIGIN	METHOD
VENDOR	MEASURE
PRICE	STEEP TIME
TASTING DATE	TEMP

🫖 TEA TYPE

☐ White ☐ Green ☐ Oolong ☐ Black ☐ Pu-erh ☐ Herbal ☐

🌿 DRY LEAF

🌿 INFUSED LEAF

☕ LIQUOR

👁 LOOK

☐ Clear ☐ Semi-Cloudy ☐ Cloudy

👃 AROMA

☐ Low ☐ Med. ☐ High Complexity

👅 PALATE

☐ Bright ☐ Smooth ☐ Light
☐ Soft ☐ Medium ☐ Medium
☐ Dull ☐ Harsh ☐ Full-Bodied

👄 FINISH

☐ Short ☐ Medium ☐ Long

😋 FLAVOR WHEEL

Earthy/ Woodsy — Smoky — Nutty/ Malty
Sweet — Metallic
Sour — Milky
Fruity — Bitter
Spicy — Mineral
Herbal — Muscatel
Vegetal — Flowery
Grassy

💬 ADDITIONAL NOTES

🧋 PREPARED WITH

☐ Milk ☐ Lemon
☐ Sugar ☐ Honey
☐ Cream ☐

☆ SCORE

/5 ☆

TEA Tasting

NAME	
ORIGIN	METHOD
VENDOR	MEASURE
PRICE	STEEP TIME
TASTING DATE	TEMP

🏷️ TEA TYPE

☐ White ☐ Green ☐ Oolong ☐ Black ☐ Pu-erh ☐ Herbal ☐

🌿 DRY LEAF   🌿 INFUSED LEAF

☕ LIQUOR

LOOK
☐ Clear ☐ Semi-Cloudy ☐ Cloudy
_____
_____

AROMA
☐ Low ☐ Med. ☐ High Complexity
_____
_____
_____
_____

PALATE
☐ Bright	☐ Smooth	☐ Light
☐ Soft	☐ Medium	☐ Medium
☐ Dull	☐ Harsh	☐ Full-Bodied
_____
_____
_____
_____
_____

FINISH
☐ Short ☐ Medium ☐ Long
_____
_____
_____

😋 FLAVOR WHEEL

Earthy / Woodsy — Smoky — Nutty / Malty
Sweet — Metallic
Sour
Fruity — Milky
Spicy — Bitter
Herbal — Mineral
Vegetal — Muscatel
Grassy — Flowery

💬 ADDITIONAL NOTES

_____
_____
_____
_____
_____
_____
_____
_____
_____
_____
_____
_____

🧊 PREPARED WITH

☐ Milk   ☐ Lemon
☐ Sugar ☐ Honey
☐ Cream ☐

⭐ SCORE

/5 ☆

TEA Tasting

NAME	
ORIGIN	METHOD
VENDOR	MEASURE
PRICE	STEEP TIME
TASTING DATE	TEMP

🔖 TEA TYPE

☐ White ☐ Green ☐ Oolong ☐ Black ☐ Pu-erh ☐ Herbal ☐

🌿 DRY LEAF

🌿 INFUSED LEAF

☕ LIQUOR

👁 LOOK
☐ Clear ☐ Semi-Cloudy ☐ Cloudy

👃 AROMA
☐ Low ☐ Med. ☐ High Complexity

👅 PALATE
☐ Bright ☐ Smooth ☐ Light
☐ Soft ☐ Medium ☐ Medium
☐ Dull ☐ Harsh ☐ Full-Bodied

👄 FINISH
☐ Short ☐ Medium ☐ Long

😋 FLAVOR WHEEL

Earthy / Woodsy Smoky Nutty / Malty
Sweet
Sour Metallic
Fruity Milky
Spicy Bitter
Herbal Mineral
Vegetal Muscatel
Grassy Flowery

💬 ADDITIONAL NOTES

🧊 PREPARED WITH

☐ Milk ☐ Lemon
☐ Sugar ☐ Honey
☐ Cream ☐

☆ SCORE

/5 ☆

11

TEA Tasting

NAME	
ORIGIN	METHOD
VENDOR	MEASURE
PRICE	STEEP TIME
TASTING DATE	TEMP

🫖 TEA TYPE

☐ White ☐ Green ☐ Oolong ☐ Black ☐ Pu-erh ☐ Herbal ☐

🌿 DRY LEAF

🌿 INFUSED LEAF

☕ LIQUOR

LOOK
☐ Clear ☐ Semi-Cloudy ☐ Cloudy

_____
_____

AROMA
☐ Low ☐ Med. ☐ High Complexity

_____
_____
_____
_____

PALATE
☐ Bright ☐ Smooth ☐ Light
☐ Soft ☐ Medium ☐ Medium
☐ Dull ☐ Harsh ☐ Full-Bodied

_____
_____
_____
_____
_____
_____

FINISH
☐ Short ☐ Medium ☐ Long

_____
_____
_____

😋 FLAVOR WHEEL

Earthy/Woodsy — Smoky — Nutty/Malty
Sweet — Metallic
Sour
Fruity — Milky
Spicy — Bitter
Herbal — Mineral
Vegetal — Muscatel
Grassy — Flowery

💬 ADDITIONAL NOTES

_____
_____
_____
_____
_____
_____
_____
_____
_____
_____

🍵 PREPARED WITH

☐ Milk ☐ Lemon
☐ Sugar ☐ Honey
☐ Cream ☐

☆ SCORE

/5 ☆

TEA Tasting

NAME	
ORIGIN	METHOD
VENDOR	MEASURE
PRICE	STEEP TIME
TASTING DATE	TEMP

🔖 TEA TYPE

☐ White ☐ Green ☐ Oolong ☐ Black ☐ Pu-erh ☐ Herbal ☐

🌱 DRY LEAF / 🌿 INFUSED LEAF

☕ LIQUOR

👁 LOOK
☐ Clear ☐ Semi-Cloudy ☐ Cloudy
_____
_____

👃 AROMA
☐ Low ☐ Med. ☐ High Complexity
_____
_____
_____
_____

👅 PALATE
☐ Bright ☐ Smooth ☐ Light
☐ Soft ☐ Medium ☐ Medium
☐ Dull ☐ Harsh ☐ Full-Bodied
_____
_____
_____
_____
_____

👄 FINISH
☐ Short ☐ Medium ☐ Long
_____
_____
_____

😊 FLAVOR WHEEL

Earthy / Woodsy — Smoky — Nutty / Malty — Metallic — Milky — Bitter — Mineral — Muscatel — Flowery — Grassy — Vegetal — Herbal — Spicy — Fruity — Sour — Sweet

💬 ADDITIONAL NOTES

🎲 PREPARED WITH

☐ Milk ☐ Lemon
☐ Sugar ☐ Honey
☐ Cream ☐

☆ SCORE

/5 ☆

13

TEA Tasting

NAME	
ORIGIN	METHOD
VENDOR	MEASURE
PRICE	STEEP TIME
TASTING DATE	TEMP

🏷️ TEA TYPE

☐ White ☐ Green ☐ Oolong ☐ Black ☐ Pu-erh ☐ Herbal ☐

🌿 DRY LEAF

🌿 INFUSED LEAF

☕ LIQUOR

👁️ LOOK

☐ Clear ☐ Semi-Cloudy ☐ Cloudy

👃 AROMA

☐ Low ☐ Med. ☐ High Complexity

👅 PALATE

☐ Bright ☐ Smooth ☐ Light
☐ Soft ☐ Medium ☐ Medium
☐ Dull ☐ Harsh ☐ Full-Bodied

👄 FINISH

☐ Short ☐ Medium ☐ Long

😋 FLAVOR WHEEL

Earthy/Woodsy Smoky Nutty/Malty
Sweet
Sour Metallic
Fruity Milky
Spicy Bitter
Herbal Mineral
Vegetal Muscatel
Grassy Flowery

💬 ADDITIONAL NOTES

🧊 PREPARED WITH

☐ Milk ☐ Lemon
☐ Sugar ☐ Honey
☐ Cream ☐

⭐ SCORE

/5 ☆

TEA Tasting

NAME	
ORIGIN	METHOD
VENDOR	MEASURE
PRICE	STEEP TIME
TASTING DATE	TEMP

🏷️ TEA TYPE

☐ White ☐ Green ☐ Oolong ☐ Black ☐ Pu-erh ☐ Herbal ☐

🌿 DRY LEAF	🌿 INFUSED LEAF

☕ LIQUOR

LOOK
☐ Clear ☐ Semi-Cloudy ☐ Cloudy
_____
_____

AROMA
☐ Low ☐ Med. ☐ High Complexity
_____
_____
_____
_____

PALATE
☐ Bright ☐ Smooth ☐ Light
☐ Soft ☐ Medium ☐ Medium
☐ Dull ☐ Harsh ☐ Full-Bodied
_____
_____
_____
_____
_____
_____
_____

FINISH
☐ Short ☐ Medium ☐ Long
_____
_____
_____

😋 FLAVOR WHEEL

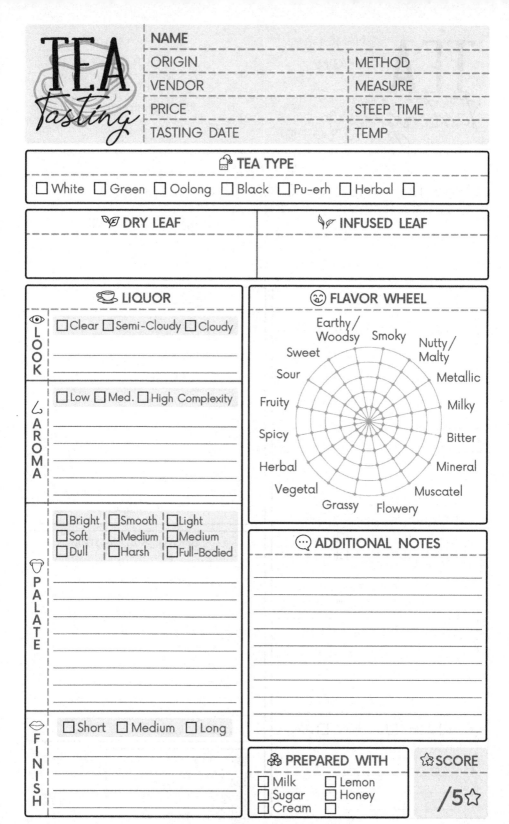

Earthy/Woodsy · Smoky · Nutty/Malty · Sweet · Sour · Metallic · Fruity · Milky · Spicy · Bitter · Herbal · Mineral · Vegetal · Muscatel · Grassy · Flowery

💬 ADDITIONAL NOTES

_____
_____
_____
_____
_____
_____
_____
_____
_____
_____

🧊 PREPARED WITH

☐ Milk ☐ Lemon
☐ Sugar ☐ Honey
☐ Cream ☐

☆ SCORE

/5 ☆

TEA Tasting

NAME	
ORIGIN	METHOD
VENDOR	MEASURE
PRICE	STEEP TIME
TASTING DATE	TEMP

🏷 TEA TYPE

☐ White ☐ Green ☐ Oolong ☐ Black ☐ Pu-erh ☐ Herbal ☐

🌿 DRY LEAF

🌿 INFUSED LEAF

☕ LIQUOR

LOOK
☐ Clear ☐ Semi-Cloudy ☐ Cloudy
_____
_____

AROMA
☐ Low ☐ Med. ☐ High Complexity
_____
_____
_____
_____
_____

PALATE
☐ Bright ☐ Smooth ☐ Light
☐ Soft ☐ Medium ☐ Medium
☐ Dull ☐ Harsh ☐ Full-Bodied
_____
_____
_____
_____
_____
_____
_____

FINISH
☐ Short ☐ Medium ☐ Long
_____
_____
_____

😋 FLAVOR WHEEL

Earthy / Woodsy — Smoky — Nutty / Malty
Sweet
Sour — Metallic
Fruity — Milky
Spicy — Bitter
Herbal — Mineral
Vegetal — Muscatel
Grassy — Flowery

💬 ADDITIONAL NOTES

🧁 PREPARED WITH

☐ Milk ☐ Lemon
☐ Sugar ☐ Honey
☐ Cream ☐

☆ SCORE

/5 ☆

16

TEA Tasting

NAME	
ORIGIN	METHOD
VENDOR	MEASURE
PRICE	STEEP TIME
TASTING DATE	TEMP

🫖 TEA TYPE

☐ White ☐ Green ☐ Oolong ☐ Black ☐ Pu-erh ☐ Herbal ☐

🌿 DRY LEAF | 🌿 INFUSED LEAF

☕ LIQUOR

LOOK 👁
☐ Clear ☐ Semi-Cloudy ☐ Cloudy
_____
_____

AROMA 👃
☐ Low ☐ Med. ☐ High Complexity
_____
_____
_____
_____

PALATE 👅
☐ Bright ☐ Smooth ☐ Light
☐ Soft ☐ Medium ☐ Medium
☐ Dull ☐ Harsh ☐ Full-Bodied
_____
_____
_____
_____
_____
_____

FINISH 👄
☐ Short ☐ Medium ☐ Long
_____
_____
_____

😋 FLAVOR WHEEL

Earthy/Woodsy Smoky Nutty/Malty
Sweet Metallic
Sour Milky
Fruity Bitter
Spicy Mineral
Herbal Muscatel
Vegetal Flowery
Grassy

💬 ADDITIONAL NOTES

_____
_____
_____
_____
_____
_____
_____
_____
_____
_____
_____

🍬 PREPARED WITH

☐ Milk ☐ Lemon
☐ Sugar ☐ Honey
☐ Cream ☐

⭐ SCORE

/5 ☆

17

TEA Tasting

NAME	
ORIGIN	METHOD
VENDOR	MEASURE
PRICE	STEEP TIME
TASTING DATE	TEMP

🫖 TEA TYPE

☐ White ☐ Green ☐ Oolong ☐ Black ☐ Pu-erh ☐ Herbal ☐

🍃 DRY LEAF

🌱 INFUSED LEAF

☕ LIQUOR

LOOK
☐ Clear ☐ Semi-Cloudy ☐ Cloudy
_____
_____

AROMA
☐ Low ☐ Med. ☐ High Complexity
_____
_____
_____
_____
_____

PALATE
☐ Bright ☐ Smooth ☐ Light
☐ Soft ☐ Medium ☐ Medium
☐ Dull ☐ Harsh ☐ Full-Bodied
_____
_____
_____
_____
_____
_____
_____

FINISH
☐ Short ☐ Medium ☐ Long
_____
_____

😋 FLAVOR WHEEL

Earthy / Woodsy
Smoky
Nutty / Malty
Sweet
Sour
Metallic
Fruity
Milky
Spicy
Bitter
Herbal
Mineral
Vegetal
Muscatel
Grassy
Flowery

💬 ADDITIONAL NOTES

🎲 PREPARED WITH

☐ Milk ☐ Lemon
☐ Sugar ☐ Honey
☐ Cream ☐

☆ SCORE

/5 ☆

TEA Tasting

NAME	
ORIGIN	METHOD
VENDOR	MEASURE
PRICE	STEEP TIME
TASTING DATE	TEMP

🔖 TEA TYPE

☐ White ☐ Green ☐ Oolong ☐ Black ☐ Pu-erh ☐ Herbal ☐

🌿 DRY LEAF

🌿 INFUSED LEAF

☕ LIQUOR

👁 LOOK

☐ Clear ☐ Semi-Cloudy ☐ Cloudy

👃 AROMA

☐ Low ☐ Med. ☐ High Complexity

👅 PALATE

☐ Bright ☐ Smooth ☐ Light
☐ Soft ☐ Medium ☐ Medium
☐ Dull ☐ Harsh ☐ Full-Bodied

👄 FINISH

☐ Short ☐ Medium ☐ Long

😋 FLAVOR WHEEL

Earthy / Woodsy
Smoky
Nutty / Malty
Sweet
Metallic
Sour
Fruity
Milky
Spicy
Bitter
Herbal
Mineral
Vegetal
Muscatel
Grassy
Flowery

💬 ADDITIONAL NOTES

🧊 PREPARED WITH

☐ Milk ☐ Lemon
☐ Sugar ☐ Honey
☐ Cream ☐

☆ SCORE

/5 ☆

19

TEA Tasting

NAME	
ORIGIN	**METHOD**
VENDOR	**MEASURE**
PRICE	**STEEP TIME**
TASTING DATE	**TEMP**

🍵 TEA TYPE

☐ White ☐ Green ☐ Oolong ☐ Black ☐ Pu-erh ☐ Herbal ☐

🌿 DRY LEAF

🌱 INFUSED LEAF

☕ LIQUOR

LOOK
☐ Clear ☐ Semi-Cloudy ☐ Cloudy
_____
_____

AROMA
☐ Low ☐ Med. ☐ High Complexity
_____
_____
_____
_____
_____

PALATE
☐ Bright ☐ Smooth ☐ Light
☐ Soft ☐ Medium ☐ Medium
☐ Dull ☐ Harsh ☐ Full-Bodied
_____
_____
_____
_____
_____
_____
_____
_____

FINISH
☐ Short ☐ Medium ☐ Long
_____
_____
_____
_____

😋 FLAVOR WHEEL

Earthy / Woodsy — Smoky — Nutty / Malty
Sweet
Sour — Metallic
Fruity — Milky
Spicy — Bitter
Herbal — Mineral
Vegetal — Muscatel
Grassy — Flowery

💬 ADDITIONAL NOTES

_____
_____
_____
_____
_____
_____
_____
_____
_____
_____
_____
_____

🧊 PREPARED WITH

☐ Milk ☐ Lemon
☐ Sugar ☐ Honey
☐ Cream ☐

☆ SCORE

/5 ☆

20

TEA Tasting

NAME	
ORIGIN	METHOD
VENDOR	MEASURE
PRICE	STEEP TIME
TASTING DATE	TEMP

🔖 TEA TYPE

☐ White   ☐ Green   ☐ Oolong   ☐ Black   ☐ Pu-erh   ☐ Herbal   ☐

🌿 DRY LEAF

🌿 INFUSED LEAF

☕ LIQUOR

👁 LOOK

☐ Clear   ☐ Semi-Cloudy   ☐ Cloudy

👃 AROMA

☐ Low   ☐ Med.   ☐ High Complexity

👅 PALATE

☐ Bright   ☐ Smooth   ☐ Light
☐ Soft   ☐ Medium   ☐ Medium
☐ Dull   ☐ Harsh   ☐ Full-Bodied

👄 FINISH

☐ Short   ☐ Medium   ☐ Long

😊 FLAVOR WHEEL

Earthy / Woodsy   Smoky   Nutty / Malty
Sweet
Sour   Metallic
Fruity   Milky
Spicy   Bitter
Herbal   Mineral
Vegetal   Muscatel
Grassy   Flowery

💬 ADDITIONAL NOTES

🧊 PREPARED WITH

☐ Milk   ☐ Lemon
☐ Sugar   ☐ Honey
☐ Cream   ☐

☆ SCORE

/5 ☆

TEA Tasting

NAME	
ORIGIN	METHOD
VENDOR	MEASURE
PRICE	STEEP TIME
TASTING DATE	TEMP

🍵 TEA TYPE

☐ White ☐ Green ☐ Oolong ☐ Black ☐ Pu-erh ☐ Herbal ☐

🌿 DRY LEAF

🌱 INFUSED LEAF

☕ LIQUOR

LOOK
☐ Clear ☐ Semi-Cloudy ☐ Cloudy

AROMA
☐ Low ☐ Med. ☐ High Complexity

PALATE
☐ Bright ☐ Smooth ☐ Light
☐ Soft ☐ Medium ☐ Medium
☐ Dull ☐ Harsh ☐ Full-Bodied

FINISH
☐ Short ☐ Medium ☐ Long

😋 FLAVOR WHEEL

Earthy / Woodsy Smoky Nutty / Malty
Sweet
Sour Metallic
Fruity Milky
Spicy Bitter
Herbal Mineral
Vegetal Muscatel
Grassy Flowery

💬 ADDITIONAL NOTES

🧊 PREPARED WITH

☐ Milk ☐ Lemon
☐ Sugar ☐ Honey
☐ Cream ☐

☆ SCORE

/5 ☆

TEA Tasting

NAME	
ORIGIN	METHOD
VENDOR	MEASURE
PRICE	STEEP TIME
TASTING DATE	TEMP

🫖 TEA TYPE

☐ White ☐ Green ☐ Oolong ☐ Black ☐ Pu-erh ☐ Herbal ☐

🌿 DRY LEAF	🌱 INFUSED LEAF

☕ LIQUOR

👁 LOOK

☐ Clear ☐ Semi-Cloudy ☐ Cloudy

_____
_____

👃 AROMA

☐ Low ☐ Med. ☐ High Complexity

_____
_____
_____
_____
_____

👅 PALATE

☐ Bright   ☐ Smooth   ☐ Light
☐ Soft   ☐ Medium   ☐ Medium
☐ Dull   ☐ Harsh   ☐ Full-Bodied

_____
_____
_____
_____
_____
_____
_____

👄 FINISH

☐ Short ☐ Medium ☐ Long

_____
_____
_____

😋 FLAVOR WHEEL

Earthy / Woodsy   Smoky   Nutty / Malty
Sweet
Sour   Metallic
Fruity   Milky
Spicy   Bitter
Herbal   Mineral
Vegetal   Muscatel
Grassy   Flowery

💬 ADDITIONAL NOTES

_____
_____
_____
_____
_____
_____
_____
_____
_____
_____
_____

🍬 PREPARED WITH

☐ Milk   ☐ Lemon
☐ Sugar   ☐ Honey
☐ Cream   ☐

☆ SCORE

/5 ☆

23

TEA Tasting

NAME	
ORIGIN	METHOD
VENDOR	MEASURE
PRICE	STEEP TIME
TASTING DATE	TEMP

🍵 TEA TYPE

☐ White ☐ Green ☐ Oolong ☐ Black ☐ Pu-erh ☐ Herbal ☐

🍃 DRY LEAF

🌱 INFUSED LEAF

☕ LIQUOR

LOOK
☐ Clear ☐ Semi-Cloudy ☐ Cloudy
_____
_____

AROMA
☐ Low ☐ Med. ☐ High Complexity
_____
_____
_____

PALATE
☐ Bright ☐ Smooth ☐ Light
☐ Soft ☐ Medium ☐ Medium
☐ Dull ☐ Harsh ☐ Full-Bodied
_____
_____
_____
_____
_____
_____

FINISH
☐ Short ☐ Medium ☐ Long
_____
_____
_____

😋 FLAVOR WHEEL

Earthy/Woodsy, Smoky, Nutty/Malty, Sweet, Metallic, Sour, Milky, Fruity, Bitter, Spicy, Mineral, Herbal, Muscatel, Vegetal, Grassy, Flowery

💬 ADDITIONAL NOTES

🧊 PREPARED WITH

☐ Milk ☐ Lemon
☐ Sugar ☐ Honey
☐ Cream ☐

⭐ SCORE

/5 ☆

TEA Tasting

NAME	
ORIGIN	METHOD
VENDOR	MEASURE
PRICE	STEEP TIME
TASTING DATE	TEMP

🏷️ TEA TYPE

☐ White ☐ Green ☐ Oolong ☐ Black ☐ Pu-erh ☐ Herbal ☐

🌿 DRY LEAF

🌱 INFUSED LEAF

☕ LIQUOR

LOOK
☐ Clear ☐ Semi-Cloudy ☐ Cloudy
_____
_____

AROMA
☐ Low ☐ Med. ☐ High Complexity
_____
_____
_____
_____

PALATE
☐ Bright ☐ Smooth ☐ Light
☐ Soft ☐ Medium ☐ Medium
☐ Dull ☐ Harsh ☐ Full-Bodied
_____
_____
_____
_____
_____

FINISH
☐ Short ☐ Medium ☐ Long
_____
_____

😋 FLAVOR WHEEL

Earthy/Woodsy — Smoky — Nutty/Malty
Sweet — Metallic
Sour — Milky
Fruity — Bitter
Spicy — Mineral
Herbal — Muscatel
Vegetal — Flowery
Grassy

💬 ADDITIONAL NOTES

🧋 PREPARED WITH

☐ Milk ☐ Lemon
☐ Sugar ☐ Honey
☐ Cream ☐

☆ SCORE

/5 ☆

TEA Tasting

NAME	
ORIGIN	METHOD
VENDOR	MEASURE
PRICE	STEEP TIME
TASTING DATE	TEMP

🫖 TEA TYPE

☐ White ☐ Green ☐ Oolong ☐ Black ☐ Pu-erh ☐ Herbal ☐

🌿 DRY LEAF

🌿 INFUSED LEAF

☕ LIQUOR

LOOK

☐ Clear ☐ Semi-Cloudy ☐ Cloudy

_____

AROMA

☐ Low ☐ Med. ☐ High Complexity

_____

PALATE

☐ Bright ☐ Smooth ☐ Light
☐ Soft ☐ Medium ☐ Medium
☐ Dull ☐ Harsh ☐ Full-Bodied

_____

FINISH

☐ Short ☐ Medium ☐ Long

_____

😊 FLAVOR WHEEL

Earthy / Woodsy · Smoky · Nutty / Malty
Sweet
Sour · Metallic
Fruity · Milky
Spicy · Bitter
Herbal · Mineral
Vegetal · Muscatel
Grassy · Flowery

💬 ADDITIONAL NOTES

🌸 PREPARED WITH

☐ Milk ☐ Lemon
☐ Sugar ☐ Honey
☐ Cream ☐

☆ SCORE

/5 ☆

26

TEA Tasting

NAME	
ORIGIN	METHOD
VENDOR	MEASURE
PRICE	STEEP TIME
TASTING DATE	TEMP

🫖 TEA TYPE

☐ White ☐ Green ☐ Oolong ☐ Black ☐ Pu-erh ☐ Herbal ☐

🌿 DRY LEAF

🌿 INFUSED LEAF

☕ LIQUOR

👁 LOOK

☐ Clear ☐ Semi-Cloudy ☐ Cloudy

_____
_____

👃 AROMA

☐ Low ☐ Med. ☐ High Complexity

_____
_____
_____
_____

👅 PALATE

☐ Bright ☐ Smooth ☐ Light
☐ Soft ☐ Medium ☐ Medium
☐ Dull ☐ Harsh ☐ Full-Bodied

_____
_____
_____
_____
_____
_____
_____

👄 FINISH

☐ Short ☐ Medium ☐ Long

_____
_____
_____

😋 FLAVOR WHEEL

Earthy / Woodsy — Smoky — Nutty / Malty
Sweet — Metallic
Sour — Milky
Fruity
Spicy — Bitter
Herbal — Mineral
Vegetal — Muscatel
Grassy — Flowery

💬 ADDITIONAL NOTES

_____
_____
_____
_____
_____
_____
_____
_____
_____
_____
_____

🧊 PREPARED WITH

☐ Milk ☐ Lemon
☐ Sugar ☐ Honey
☐ Cream ☐

☆ SCORE

/5 ☆

27

TEA Tasting

NAME	
ORIGIN	METHOD
VENDOR	MEASURE
PRICE	STEEP TIME
TASTING DATE	TEMP

🔖 TEA TYPE

☐ White ☐ Green ☐ Oolong ☐ Black ☐ Pu-erh ☐ Herbal ☐

🍃 DRY LEAF

🍃 INFUSED LEAF

☕ LIQUOR

👁 LOOK

☐ Clear ☐ Semi-Cloudy ☐ Cloudy

_____
_____

👃 AROMA

☐ Low ☐ Med. ☐ High Complexity

_____
_____
_____
_____

🥄 PALATE

☐ Bright ☐ Smooth ☐ Light
☐ Soft ☐ Medium ☐ Medium
☐ Dull ☐ Harsh ☐ Full-Bodied

_____
_____
_____
_____
_____
_____
_____

👄 FINISH

☐ Short ☐ Medium ☐ Long

_____
_____
_____

☺ FLAVOR WHEEL

Earthy/Woodsy Smoky Nutty/Malty
Sweet
Sour   Metallic
Fruity   Milky
Spicy   Bitter
Herbal   Mineral
Vegetal   Muscatel
Grassy Flowery

💬 ADDITIONAL NOTES

_____
_____
_____
_____
_____
_____
_____
_____
_____
_____
_____
_____

🧊 PREPARED WITH

☐ Milk ☐ Lemon
☐ Sugar ☐ Honey
☐ Cream ☐

☆ SCORE

/5 ☆

TEA Tasting

NAME	
ORIGIN	METHOD
VENDOR	MEASURE
PRICE	STEEP TIME
TASTING DATE	TEMP

🔒 TEA TYPE

☐ White ☐ Green ☐ Oolong ☐ Black ☐ Pu-erh ☐ Herbal ☐

🌿 DRY LEAF

🌿 INFUSED LEAF

☕ LIQUOR

👁 LOOK

☐ Clear ☐ Semi-Cloudy ☐ Cloudy
_____
_____

👃 AROMA

☐ Low ☐ Med. ☐ High Complexity
_____
_____
_____
_____

👅 PALATE

☐ Bright ☐ Smooth ☐ Light
☐ Soft ☐ Medium ☐ Medium
☐ Dull ☐ Harsh ☐ Full-Bodied
_____
_____
_____
_____
_____
_____

👄 FINISH

☐ Short ☐ Medium ☐ Long
_____
_____
_____

😋 FLAVOR WHEEL

Earthy / Woodsy, Smoky, Nutty / Malty, Sweet, Sour, Metallic, Fruity, Milky, Spicy, Bitter, Herbal, Mineral, Vegetal, Muscatel, Grassy, Flowery

💬 ADDITIONAL NOTES

_____
_____
_____
_____
_____
_____
_____
_____
_____
_____

🧊 PREPARED WITH

☐ Milk ☐ Lemon
☐ Sugar ☐ Honey
☐ Cream ☐

☆ SCORE

/5 ☆

TEA Tasting

NAME	
ORIGIN	METHOD
VENDOR	MEASURE
PRICE	STEEP TIME
TASTING DATE	TEMP

🍵 TEA TYPE

☐ White ☐ Green ☐ Oolong ☐ Black ☐ Pu-erh ☐ Herbal ☐

🌿 DRY LEAF

🌿 INFUSED LEAF

☕ LIQUOR

LOOK

☐ Clear ☐ Semi-Cloudy ☐ Cloudy
_____
_____

AROMA

☐ Low ☐ Med. ☐ High Complexity
_____
_____
_____
_____
_____

PALATE

☐ Bright ☐ Smooth ☐ Light
☐ Soft ☐ Medium ☐ Medium
☐ Dull ☐ Harsh ☐ Full-Bodied
_____
_____
_____
_____
_____
_____

FINISH

☐ Short ☐ Medium ☐ Long
_____
_____
_____

😋 FLAVOR WHEEL

Earthy/Woodsy
Smoky
Nutty/Malty
Sweet
Metallic
Sour
Milky
Fruity
Bitter
Spicy
Mineral
Herbal
Muscatel
Vegetal
Grassy
Flowery

💬 ADDITIONAL NOTES

_____
_____
_____
_____
_____
_____
_____
_____
_____
_____
_____

🎲 PREPARED WITH

☐ Milk ☐ Lemon
☐ Sugar ☐ Honey
☐ Cream ☐

☆ SCORE

/5 ☆

30

TEA Tasting

NAME	
ORIGIN	METHOD
VENDOR	MEASURE
PRICE	STEEP TIME
TASTING DATE	TEMP

🏷️ TEA TYPE

☐ White ☐ Green ☐ Oolong ☐ Black ☐ Pu-erh ☐ Herbal ☐

🌿 DRY LEAF

🌿 INFUSED LEAF

☕ LIQUOR

LOOK
☐ Clear ☐ Semi-Cloudy ☐ Cloudy
_____
_____

AROMA
☐ Low ☐ Med. ☐ High Complexity
_____
_____
_____
_____

PALATE
☐ Bright ☐ Smooth ☐ Light
☐ Soft ☐ Medium ☐ Medium
☐ Dull ☐ Harsh ☐ Full-Bodied
_____
_____
_____
_____
_____
_____

FINISH
☐ Short ☐ Medium ☐ Long
_____
_____
_____

😋 FLAVOR WHEEL

Earthy/Woodsy Smoky Nutty/Malty
Sweet
Sour Metallic
Fruity Milky
Spicy Bitter
Herbal Mineral
Vegetal Muscatel
Grassy Flowery

💬 ADDITIONAL NOTES

🍬 PREPARED WITH

☐ Milk ☐ Lemon
☐ Sugar ☐ Honey
☐ Cream ☐

☆ SCORE

/5 ☆

31

TEA Tasting

NAME	
ORIGIN	METHOD
VENDOR	MEASURE
PRICE	STEEP TIME
TASTING DATE	TEMP

🫖 TEA TYPE

☐ White ☐ Green ☐ Oolong ☐ Black ☐ Pu-erh ☐ Herbal ☐

🌿 DRY LEAF

🌿 INFUSED LEAF

☕ LIQUOR

LOOK

☐ Clear ☐ Semi-Cloudy ☐ Cloudy

_____

AROMA

☐ Low ☐ Med. ☐ High Complexity

_____

PALATE

☐ Bright ☐ Smooth ☐ Light
☐ Soft ☐ Medium ☐ Medium
☐ Dull ☐ Harsh ☐ Full-Bodied

_____

FINISH

☐ Short ☐ Medium ☐ Long

_____

😋 FLAVOR WHEEL

Earthy / Woodsy · Smoky · Nutty / Malty · Sweet · Metallic · Sour · Fruity · Milky · Spicy · Bitter · Herbal · Mineral · Vegetal · Muscatel · Grassy · Flowery

💬 ADDITIONAL NOTES

🧊 PREPARED WITH

☐ Milk ☐ Lemon
☐ Sugar ☐ Honey
☐ Cream ☐

☆ SCORE

/5 ☆

TEA Tasting

NAME	
ORIGIN	METHOD
VENDOR	MEASURE
PRICE	STEEP TIME
TASTING DATE	TEMP

🏷 TEA TYPE

☐ White ☐ Green ☐ Oolong ☐ Black ☐ Pu-erh ☐ Herbal ☐

🌿 DRY LEAF	🌱 INFUSED LEAF

☕ LIQUOR

👁 LOOK

☐ Clear ☐ Semi-Cloudy ☐ Cloudy

_____

👃 AROMA

☐ Low ☐ Med. ☐ High Complexity

_____

👅 PALATE

☐ Bright ☐ Smooth ☐ Light
☐ Soft ☐ Medium ☐ Medium
☐ Dull ☐ Harsh ☐ Full-Bodied

_____

👄 FINISH

☐ Short ☐ Medium ☐ Long

_____

☺ FLAVOR WHEEL

Earthy / Woodsy Smoky Nutty / Malty
Sweet Metallic
Sour Milky
Fruity Bitter
Spicy Mineral
Herbal Muscatel
Vegetal Flowery
Grassy

💬 ADDITIONAL NOTES

_____

🧊 PREPARED WITH

☐ Milk ☐ Lemon
☐ Sugar ☐ Honey
☐ Cream ☐

☆ SCORE

/5 ☆

TEA
Tasting

NAME	
ORIGIN	METHOD
VENDOR	MEASURE
PRICE	STEEP TIME
TASTING DATE	TEMP

🍵 TEA TYPE

☐ White ☐ Green ☐ Oolong ☐ Black ☐ Pu-erh ☐ Herbal ☐

🌿 DRY LEAF

🌱 INFUSED LEAF

☕ LIQUOR

👁 LOOK
☐ Clear ☐ Semi-Cloudy ☐ Cloudy
_____
_____

👃 AROMA
☐ Low ☐ Med. ☐ High Complexity
_____
_____
_____
_____
_____

👅 PALATE
☐ Bright ☐ Smooth ☐ Light
☐ Soft ☐ Medium ☐ Medium
☐ Dull ☐ Harsh ☐ Full-Bodied
_____
_____
_____
_____
_____
_____

👄 FINISH
☐ Short ☐ Medium ☐ Long
_____
_____
_____

😋 FLAVOR WHEEL

Earthy / Woodsy
Smoky
Nutty / Malty
Sweet
Sour
Metallic
Fruity
Milky
Spicy
Bitter
Herbal
Mineral
Vegetal
Muscatel
Grassy
Flowery

💬 ADDITIONAL NOTES

🎲 PREPARED WITH

☐ Milk ☐ Lemon
☐ Sugar ☐ Honey
☐ Cream ☐

☆ SCORE

/5 ☆

34

TEA Tasting

NAME	
ORIGIN	METHOD
VENDOR	MEASURE
PRICE	STEEP TIME
TASTING DATE	TEMP

🫖 TEA TYPE

☐ White ☐ Green ☐ Oolong ☐ Black ☐ Pu-erh ☐ Herbal ☐

🌿 DRY LEAF	🌱 INFUSED LEAF

☕ LIQUOR

👁 LOOK
☐ Clear ☐ Semi-Cloudy ☐ Cloudy
_____

👃 AROMA
☐ Low ☐ Med. ☐ High Complexity
_____
_____
_____
_____

👅 PALATE
☐ Bright ☐ Smooth ☐ Light
☐ Soft ☐ Medium ☐ Medium
☐ Dull ☐ Harsh ☐ Full-Bodied
_____
_____
_____
_____
_____
_____

👄 FINISH
☐ Short ☐ Medium ☐ Long
_____
_____
_____

😋 FLAVOR WHEEL

Earthy/Woodsy Smoky Nutty/Malty
Sweet Metallic
Sour Milky
Fruity Bitter
Spicy Mineral
Herbal Muscatel
Vegetal Flowery
Grassy

💬 ADDITIONAL NOTES

_____
_____
_____
_____
_____
_____
_____
_____
_____
_____

🧊 PREPARED WITH

☐ Milk ☐ Lemon
☐ Sugar ☐ Honey
☐ Cream ☐

☆ SCORE

/5 ☆

TEA Tasting

NAME			
ORIGIN		METHOD	
VENDOR		MEASURE	
PRICE		STEEP TIME	
TASTING DATE		TEMP	

🫖 TEA TYPE

☐ White ☐ Green ☐ Oolong ☐ Black ☐ Pu-erh ☐ Herbal ☐

🌿 DRY LEAF

🍃 INFUSED LEAF

☕ LIQUOR

👁 LOOK
☐ Clear ☐ Semi-Cloudy ☐ Cloudy
_____
_____

👃 AROMA
☐ Low ☐ Med. ☐ High Complexity
_____
_____
_____
_____

👅 PALATE
☐ Bright ☐ Smooth ☐ Light
☐ Soft ☐ Medium ☐ Medium
☐ Dull ☐ Harsh ☐ Full-Bodied
_____
_____
_____
_____
_____
_____

👄 FINISH
☐ Short ☐ Medium ☐ Long
_____
_____
_____

😋 FLAVOR WHEEL

Earthy/Woodsy Smoky Nutty/Malty
Sweet
Sour Metallic
Fruity Milky
Spicy Bitter
Herbal Mineral
Vegetal Muscatel
Grassy Flowery

💬 ADDITIONAL NOTES

_____
_____
_____
_____
_____
_____
_____
_____
_____
_____

🧊 PREPARED WITH

☐ Milk ☐ Lemon
☐ Sugar ☐ Honey
☐ Cream ☐

☆ SCORE

/5 ☆

36

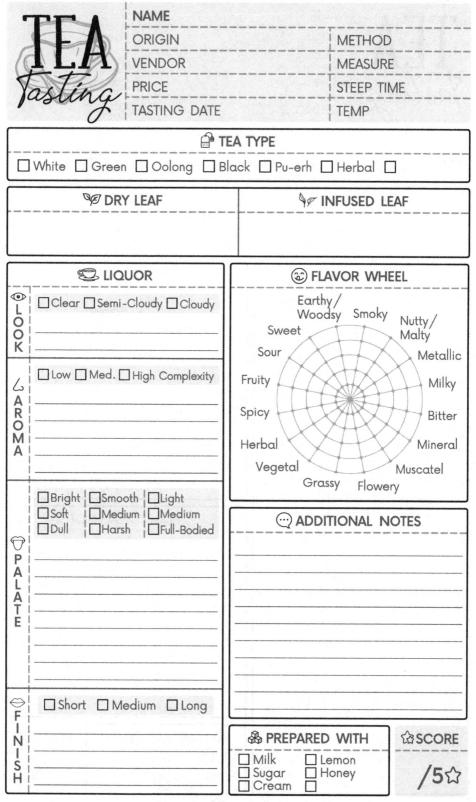

TEA Tasting

NAME	
ORIGIN	METHOD
VENDOR	MEASURE
PRICE	STEEP TIME
TASTING DATE	TEMP

🔖 TEA TYPE

☐ White ☐ Green ☐ Oolong ☐ Black ☐ Pu-erh ☐ Herbal ☐

🌱 DRY LEAF

🌿 INFUSED LEAF

☕ LIQUOR

👁 LOOK
☐ Clear ☐ Semi-Cloudy ☐ Cloudy

👃 AROMA
☐ Low ☐ Med. ☐ High Complexity

👅 PALATE
☐ Bright ☐ Smooth ☐ Light
☐ Soft ☐ Medium ☐ Medium
☐ Dull ☐ Harsh ☐ Full-Bodied

👄 FINISH
☐ Short ☐ Medium ☐ Long

😋 FLAVOR WHEEL

Earthy/Woodsy — Smoky — Nutty/Malty
Sweet
Sour — Metallic
Fruity — Milky
Spicy — Bitter
Herbal — Mineral
Vegetal — Muscatel
Grassy — Flowery

💬 ADDITIONAL NOTES

🧊 PREPARED WITH

☐ Milk ☐ Lemon
☐ Sugar ☐ Honey
☐ Cream ☐

☆ SCORE

/5 ☆

37

TEA Tasting

NAME	
ORIGIN	METHOD
VENDOR	MEASURE
PRICE	STEEP TIME
TASTING DATE	TEMP

🫖 TEA TYPE

☐ White ☐ Green ☐ Oolong ☐ Black ☐ Pu-erh ☐ Herbal ☐

🍃 DRY LEAF

🌿 INFUSED LEAF

☕ LIQUOR

👁 LOOK

☐ Clear ☐ Semi-Cloudy ☐ Cloudy

_____

👃 AROMA

☐ Low ☐ Med. ☐ High Complexity

_____
_____
_____

👅 PALATE

☐ Bright ☐ Smooth ☐ Light
☐ Soft ☐ Medium ☐ Medium
☐ Dull ☐ Harsh ☐ Full-Bodied

_____
_____
_____
_____
_____
_____
_____

👄 FINISH

☐ Short ☐ Medium ☐ Long

_____
_____
_____

😋 FLAVOR WHEEL

Earthy / Woodsy Smoky Nutty / Malty
Sweet
Sour Metallic
Fruity Milky
Spicy Bitter
Herbal Mineral
Vegetal Muscatel
Grassy Flowery

💬 ADDITIONAL NOTES

_____
_____
_____
_____
_____
_____
_____
_____
_____
_____
_____

♣ PREPARED WITH

☐ Milk ☐ Lemon
☐ Sugar ☐ Honey
☐ Cream ☐

☆ SCORE

/5 ☆

TEA Tasting

NAME	
ORIGIN	METHOD
VENDOR	MEASURE
PRICE	STEEP TIME
TASTING DATE	TEMP

🏷️ TEA TYPE

☐ White ☐ Green ☐ Oolong ☐ Black ☐ Pu-erh ☐ Herbal ☐

🌿 DRY LEAF

🌱 INFUSED LEAF

☕ LIQUOR

LOOK
☐ Clear ☐ Semi-Cloudy ☐ Cloudy
_____
_____

AROMA
☐ Low ☐ Med. ☐ High Complexity
_____
_____
_____
_____

PALATE
☐ Bright ☐ Smooth ☐ Light
☐ Soft ☐ Medium ☐ Medium
☐ Dull ☐ Harsh ☐ Full-Bodied
_____
_____
_____
_____
_____
_____

FINISH
☐ Short ☐ Medium ☐ Long
_____
_____
_____

😊 FLAVOR WHEEL

Earthy / Woodsy · Smoky · Nutty / Malty
Sweet · Metallic
Sour · Milky
Fruity
Spicy · Bitter
Herbal · Mineral
Vegetal · Muscatel
Grassy · Flowery

💬 ADDITIONAL NOTES

_____
_____
_____
_____
_____
_____
_____
_____
_____
_____
_____

❄️ PREPARED WITH

☐ Milk ☐ Lemon
☐ Sugar ☐ Honey
☐ Cream ☐

☆ SCORE

/5 ☆

39

TEA Tasting

NAME	
ORIGIN	METHOD
VENDOR	MEASURE
PRICE	STEEP TIME
TASTING DATE	TEMP

🫖 TEA TYPE

☐ White ☐ Green ☐ Oolong ☐ Black ☐ Pu-erh ☐ Herbal ☐

🌱 DRY LEAF

🌱 INFUSED LEAF

☕ LIQUOR

LOOK 👁
☐ Clear ☐ Semi-Cloudy ☐ Cloudy
_____
_____

AROMA 👃
☐ Low ☐ Med. ☐ High Complexity
_____
_____
_____
_____

PALATE 👅
☐ Bright ☐ Smooth ☐ Light
☐ Soft ☐ Medium ☐ Medium
☐ Dull ☐ Harsh ☐ Full-Bodied
_____
_____
_____
_____
_____

FINISH 👄
☐ Short ☐ Medium ☐ Long
_____
_____
_____

😋 FLAVOR WHEEL

Earthy / Woodsy · Smoky · Nutty / Malty
Sweet
Sour · Metallic
Fruity · Milky
Spicy · Bitter
Herbal · Mineral
Vegetal · Muscatel
Grassy · Flowery

💬 ADDITIONAL NOTES

_____
_____
_____
_____
_____
_____
_____
_____
_____
_____
_____
_____
_____

🧊 PREPARED WITH

☐ Milk ☐ Lemon
☐ Sugar ☐ Honey
☐ Cream ☐

⭐ SCORE

/5 ☆

40

TEA Tasting

NAME	
ORIGIN	METHOD
VENDOR	MEASURE
PRICE	STEEP TIME
TASTING DATE	TEMP

🫖 TEA TYPE

☐ White ☐ Green ☐ Oolong ☐ Black ☐ Pu-erh ☐ Herbal ☐

🍃 DRY LEAF

🌱 INFUSED LEAF

☕ LIQUOR

👁 LOOK
☐ Clear ☐ Semi-Cloudy ☐ Cloudy

_____
_____

👃 AROMA
☐ Low ☐ Med. ☐ High Complexity

_____
_____
_____
_____

🫗 PALATE
☐ Bright ☐ Smooth ☐ Light
☐ Soft ☐ Medium ☐ Medium
☐ Dull ☐ Harsh ☐ Full-Bodied

_____
_____
_____
_____
_____
_____

👄 FINISH
☐ Short ☐ Medium ☐ Long

_____
_____
_____

😋 FLAVOR WHEEL

Earthy/Woodsy Smoky Nutty/Malty
Sweet Metallic
Sour
Fruity Milky
Spicy Bitter
Herbal Mineral
Vegetal Muscatel
Grassy Flowery

💬 ADDITIONAL NOTES

_____
_____
_____
_____
_____
_____
_____
_____
_____
_____

🧊 PREPARED WITH

☐ Milk ☐ Lemon
☐ Sugar ☐ Honey
☐ Cream ☐

☆ SCORE

/5 ☆

41

TEA Tasting

NAME	
ORIGIN	METHOD
VENDOR	MEASURE
PRICE	STEEP TIME
TASTING DATE	TEMP

🍵 TEA TYPE

☐ White ☐ Green ☐ Oolong ☐ Black ☐ Pu-erh ☐ Herbal ☐

🌿 DRY LEAF

🌱 INFUSED LEAF

☕ LIQUOR

👁 LOOK
☐ Clear ☐ Semi-Cloudy ☐ Cloudy

👃 AROMA
☐ Low ☐ Med. ☐ High Complexity

👅 PALATE
☐ Bright ☐ Smooth ☐ Light
☐ Soft ☐ Medium ☐ Medium
☐ Dull ☐ Harsh ☐ Full-Bodied

👄 FINISH
☐ Short ☐ Medium ☐ Long

😋 FLAVOR WHEEL

Earthy/Woodsy Smoky Nutty/Malty
Sweet Metallic
Sour Milky
Fruity Bitter
Spicy Mineral
Herbal Muscatel
Vegetal Flowery
Grassy

💬 ADDITIONAL NOTES

🎲 PREPARED WITH

☐ Milk ☐ Lemon
☐ Sugar ☐ Honey
☐ Cream ☐

☆ SCORE

/5 ☆

TEA Tasting

NAME	
ORIGIN	METHOD
VENDOR	MEASURE
PRICE	STEEP TIME
TASTING DATE	TEMP

🏷 TEA TYPE

☐ White ☐ Green ☐ Oolong ☐ Black ☐ Pu-erh ☐ Herbal ☐

🌿 DRY LEAF

🌿 INFUSED LEAF

☕ LIQUOR

👁 LOOK

☐ Clear ☐ Semi-Cloudy ☐ Cloudy

_____
_____

👃 AROMA

☐ Low ☐ Med. ☐ High Complexity

_____
_____
_____
_____

👅 PALATE

☐ Bright ☐ Smooth ☐ Light
☐ Soft ☐ Medium ☐ Medium
☐ Dull ☐ Harsh ☐ Full-Bodied

_____
_____
_____
_____
_____
_____

👄 FINISH

☐ Short ☐ Medium ☐ Long

_____
_____
_____

😋 FLAVOR WHEEL

Earthy/Woodsy Smoky Nutty/Malty
Sweet
Sour Metallic
Fruity Milky
Spicy Bitter
Herbal Mineral
Vegetal Muscatel
Grassy Flowery

💬 ADDITIONAL NOTES

_____
_____
_____
_____
_____
_____
_____
_____
_____
_____

🧊 PREPARED WITH

☐ Milk ☐ Lemon
☐ Sugar ☐ Honey
☐ Cream ☐

☆ SCORE

/5 ☆

TEA
Tasting

NAME	
ORIGIN	METHOD
VENDOR	MEASURE
PRICE	STEEP TIME
TASTING DATE	TEMP

🔖 TEA TYPE

☐ White ☐ Green ☐ Oolong ☐ Black ☐ Pu-erh ☐ Herbal ☐

🌱 DRY LEAF	🌿 INFUSED LEAF

☕ LIQUOR

👁 LOOK

☐ Clear ☐ Semi-Cloudy ☐ Cloudy
_____
_____

👃 AROMA

☐ Low ☐ Med. ☐ High Complexity
_____
_____
_____
_____

👅 PALATE

☐ Bright ☐ Smooth ☐ Light
☐ Soft ☐ Medium ☐ Medium
☐ Dull ☐ Harsh ☐ Full-Bodied
_____
_____
_____
_____
_____
_____

👄 FINISH

☐ Short ☐ Medium ☐ Long
_____
_____
_____

😋 FLAVOR WHEEL

Earthy / Woodsy · Smoky · Nutty / Malty
Sweet · Metallic
Sour · Milky
Fruity · Bitter
Spicy · Mineral
Herbal · Muscatel
Vegetal · Flowery
Grassy

💬 ADDITIONAL NOTES

_____
_____
_____
_____
_____
_____
_____
_____
_____
_____
_____
_____
_____
_____

🍀 PREPARED WITH

☐ Milk ☐ Lemon
☐ Sugar ☐ Honey
☐ Cream ☐

☆ SCORE

/5 ☆

TEA
Tasting

NAME	
ORIGIN	METHOD
VENDOR	MEASURE
PRICE	STEEP TIME
TASTING DATE	TEMP

🫖 TEA TYPE

☐ White ☐ Green ☐ Oolong ☐ Black ☐ Pu-erh ☐ Herbal ☐

🌿 DRY LEAF

🌱 INFUSED LEAF

☕ LIQUOR

👁 LOOK

☐ Clear ☐ Semi-Cloudy ☐ Cloudy
_____
_____

👃 AROMA

☐ Low ☐ Med. ☐ High Complexity
_____
_____
_____
_____

👅 PALATE

☐ Bright ☐ Smooth ☐ Light
☐ Soft ☐ Medium ☐ Medium
☐ Dull ☐ Harsh ☐ Full-Bodied
_____
_____
_____
_____
_____
_____
_____

👄 FINISH

☐ Short ☐ Medium ☐ Long
_____
_____
_____

😋 FLAVOR WHEEL

Earthy/Woodsy Smoky Nutty/Malty
Sweet
Sour Metallic
Fruity Milky
Spicy Bitter
Herbal Mineral
Vegetal Muscatel
Grassy Flowery

💬 ADDITIONAL NOTES

_____
_____
_____
_____
_____
_____
_____
_____
_____
_____
_____

🍬 PREPARED WITH

☐ Milk ☐ Lemon
☐ Sugar ☐ Honey
☐ Cream ☐

☆ SCORE

/5 ☆

TEA Tasting

NAME	
ORIGIN	METHOD
VENDOR	MEASURE
PRICE	STEEP TIME
TASTING DATE	TEMP

🔖 TEA TYPE

☐ White ☐ Green ☐ Oolong ☐ Black ☐ Pu-erh ☐ Herbal ☐

🌿 DRY LEAF

🌱 INFUSED LEAF

☕ LIQUOR

👁 LOOK

☐ Clear ☐ Semi-Cloudy ☐ Cloudy

👃 AROMA

☐ Low ☐ Med. ☐ High Complexity

🥃 PALATE

☐ Bright ☐ Smooth ☐ Light
☐ Soft ☐ Medium ☐ Medium
☐ Dull ☐ Harsh ☐ Full-Bodied

👄 FINISH

☐ Short ☐ Medium ☐ Long

😋 FLAVOR WHEEL

Earthy/Woodsy Smoky Nutty/Malty
Sweet
Sour Metallic
Fruity Milky
Spicy Bitter
Herbal Mineral
Vegetal Muscatel
Grassy Flowery

💬 ADDITIONAL NOTES

🧊 PREPARED WITH

☐ Milk ☐ Lemon
☐ Sugar ☐ Honey
☐ Cream ☐

⭐ SCORE

/5 ☆

TEA Tasting

NAME	
ORIGIN	METHOD
VENDOR	MEASURE
PRICE	STEEP TIME
TASTING DATE	TEMP

🍵 TEA TYPE

☐ White ☐ Green ☐ Oolong ☐ Black ☐ Pu-erh ☐ Herbal ☐

🌿 DRY LEAF

🌿 INFUSED LEAF

☕ LIQUOR

LOOK

☐ Clear ☐ Semi-Cloudy ☐ Cloudy
_____
_____

AROMA

☐ Low ☐ Med. ☐ High Complexity
_____
_____
_____
_____

PALATE

☐ Bright ☐ Smooth ☐ Light
☐ Soft ☐ Medium ☐ Medium
☐ Dull ☐ Harsh ☐ Full-Bodied
_____
_____
_____
_____
_____
_____
_____

FINISH

☐ Short ☐ Medium ☐ Long
_____
_____
_____

😋 FLAVOR WHEEL

Earthy/Woodsy Smoky Nutty/Malty
Sweet
Sour   Metallic
Fruity   Milky
Spicy   Bitter
Herbal   Mineral
Vegetal   Muscatel
Grassy Flowery

💬 ADDITIONAL NOTES

_____
_____
_____
_____
_____
_____
_____
_____
_____
_____

🧊 PREPARED WITH

☐ Milk ☐ Lemon
☐ Sugar ☐ Honey
☐ Cream ☐

☆ SCORE

/5☆

47

TEA Tasting

NAME	
ORIGIN	METHOD
VENDOR	MEASURE
PRICE	STEEP TIME
TASTING DATE	TEMP

🏷️ TEA TYPE

☐ White   ☐ Green   ☐ Oolong   ☐ Black   ☐ Pu-erh   ☐ Herbal   ☐

🌿 DRY LEAF

🌱 INFUSED LEAF

☕ LIQUOR

LOOK
☐ Clear ☐ Semi-Cloudy ☐ Cloudy
_____
_____

AROMA
☐ Low ☐ Med. ☐ High Complexity
_____
_____
_____
_____
_____

PALATE
☐ Bright ☐ Smooth ☐ Light
☐ Soft   ☐ Medium ☐ Medium
☐ Dull   ☐ Harsh   ☐ Full-Bodied
_____
_____
_____
_____
_____
_____
_____

FINISH
☐ Short ☐ Medium ☐ Long
_____
_____
_____

😋 FLAVOR WHEEL

Earthy / Woodsy   Smoky   Nutty / Malty
Sweet
Sour   Metallic
Fruity   Milky
Spicy   Bitter
Herbal   Mineral
Vegetal   Muscatel
Grassy   Flowery

💬 ADDITIONAL NOTES

_____
_____
_____
_____
_____
_____
_____
_____
_____
_____

🧊 PREPARED WITH

☐ Milk   ☐ Lemon
☐ Sugar   ☐ Honey
☐ Cream   ☐

⭐ SCORE

/5 ☆

48

TEA Tasting

NAME	
ORIGIN	METHOD
VENDOR	MEASURE
PRICE	STEEP TIME
TASTING DATE	TEMP

🏷️ TEA TYPE

☐ White ☐ Green ☐ Oolong ☐ Black ☐ Pu-erh ☐ Herbal ☐

🌿 DRY LEAF

🍃 INFUSED LEAF

☕ LIQUOR

LOOK

☐ Clear ☐ Semi-Cloudy ☐ Cloudy
_____
_____

AROMA

☐ Low ☐ Med. ☐ High Complexity
_____
_____
_____
_____

PALATE

☐ Bright ☐ Smooth ☐ Light
☐ Soft ☐ Medium ☐ Medium
☐ Dull ☐ Harsh ☐ Full-Bodied
_____
_____
_____
_____
_____

FINISH

☐ Short ☐ Medium ☐ Long
_____
_____
_____

😋 FLAVOR WHEEL

Earthy / Woodsy · Smoky · Nutty / Malty
Sweet · Metallic
Sour · Milky
Fruity · Bitter
Spicy · Mineral
Herbal · Muscatel
Vegetal · Flowery
Grassy

💬 ADDITIONAL NOTES

_____
_____
_____
_____
_____
_____
_____
_____
_____
_____
_____
_____
_____

🧊 PREPARED WITH

☐ Milk ☐ Lemon
☐ Sugar ☐ Honey
☐ Cream ☐

☆ SCORE

/5 ☆

49

TEA Tasting

NAME	
ORIGIN	METHOD
VENDOR	MEASURE
PRICE	STEEP TIME
TASTING DATE	TEMP

🫖 TEA TYPE

☐ White ☐ Green ☐ Oolong ☐ Black ☐ Pu-erh ☐ Herbal ☐

🌿 DRY LEAF
🌿 INFUSED LEAF

☕ LIQUOR

👁 LOOK

☐ Clear ☐ Semi-Cloudy ☐ Cloudy

👃 AROMA

☐ Low ☐ Med. ☐ High Complexity

🫖 PALATE

☐ Bright ☐ Smooth ☐ Light
☐ Soft ☐ Medium ☐ Medium
☐ Dull ☐ Harsh ☐ Full-Bodied

👄 FINISH

☐ Short ☐ Medium ☐ Long

😋 FLAVOR WHEEL

Earthy/Woodsy Smoky Nutty/Malty
Sweet
Sour Metallic
Fruity Milky
Spicy Bitter
Herbal Mineral
Vegetal Muscatel
Grassy Flowery

💬 ADDITIONAL NOTES

🧊 PREPARED WITH

☐ Milk ☐ Lemon
☐ Sugar ☐ Honey
☐ Cream ☐

☆ SCORE

/5☆

TEA Tasting

NAME	
ORIGIN	METHOD
VENDOR	MEASURE
PRICE	STEEP TIME
TASTING DATE	TEMP

🔒 TEA TYPE

☐ White ☐ Green ☐ Oolong ☐ Black ☐ Pu-erh ☐ Herbal ☐

🌿 DRY LEAF

🌿 INFUSED LEAF

☕ LIQUOR

LOOK

☐ Clear ☐ Semi-Cloudy ☐ Cloudy
_____
_____

AROMA

☐ Low ☐ Med. ☐ High Complexity
_____
_____
_____
_____

PALATE

☐ Bright ☐ Smooth ☐ Light
☐ Soft   ☐ Medium ☐ Medium
☐ Dull   ☐ Harsh   ☐ Full-Bodied
_____
_____
_____
_____
_____
_____

FINISH

☐ Short ☐ Medium ☐ Long
_____
_____
_____

😋 FLAVOR WHEEL

Earthy/Woodsy Smoky Nutty/Malty
Sweet
Sour
Fruity
Spicy
Herbal
Vegetal
Grassy Flowery
Metallic
Milky
Bitter
Mineral
Muscatel

💬 ADDITIONAL NOTES

_____
_____
_____
_____
_____
_____
_____
_____
_____
_____

🧊 PREPARED WITH

☐ Milk   ☐ Lemon
☐ Sugar   ☐ Honey
☐ Cream   ☐

☆ SCORE

/5 ☆

TEA
Tasting

NAME

ORIGIN | METHOD

VENDOR | MEASURE

PRICE | STEEP TIME

TASTING DATE | TEMP

🏷 TEA TYPE

☐ White ☐ Green ☐ Oolong ☐ Black ☐ Pu-erh ☐ Herbal ☐

🌿 DRY LEAF | 🌿 INFUSED LEAF

☕ LIQUOR

👁 LOOK
☐ Clear ☐ Semi-Cloudy ☐ Cloudy

_____

_____

👃 AROMA
☐ Low ☐ Med. ☐ High Complexity

_____

_____

_____

_____

👅 PALATE
☐ Bright ☐ Smooth ☐ Light
☐ Soft ☐ Medium ☐ Medium
☐ Dull ☐ Harsh ☐ Full-Bodied

_____

_____

_____

_____

_____

👄 FINISH
☐ Short ☐ Medium ☐ Long

_____

_____

_____

😋 FLAVOR WHEEL

Earthy / Woodsy   Smoky   Nutty / Malty

Sweet

Sour   Metallic

Fruity   Milky

Spicy   Bitter

Herbal   Mineral

Vegetal   Muscatel

Grassy   Flowery

💬 ADDITIONAL NOTES

🧊 PREPARED WITH

☐ Milk   ☐ Lemon
☐ Sugar   ☐ Honey
☐ Cream   ☐

☆ SCORE

/5 ☆

TEA Tasting

NAME	
ORIGIN	METHOD
VENDOR	MEASURE
PRICE	STEEP TIME
TASTING DATE	TEMP

🫖 TEA TYPE

☐ White   ☐ Green   ☐ Oolong   ☐ Black   ☐ Pu-erh   ☐ Herbal   ☐

🌿 DRY LEAF | 🌱 INFUSED LEAF

☕ LIQUOR

👁 LOOK
☐ Clear ☐ Semi-Cloudy ☐ Cloudy
_____
_____

👃 AROMA
☐ Low ☐ Med. ☐ High Complexity
_____
_____
_____
_____

👅 PALATE
☐ Bright   ☐ Smooth   ☐ Light
☐ Soft   ☐ Medium   ☐ Medium
☐ Dull   ☐ Harsh   ☐ Full-Bodied
_____
_____
_____
_____
_____
_____

👄 FINISH
☐ Short ☐ Medium ☐ Long
_____
_____
_____

😋 FLAVOR WHEEL

Earthy/Woodsy   Smoky   Nutty/Malty
Sweet   Metallic
Sour
Fruity   Milky
Spicy   Bitter
Herbal   Mineral
Vegetal   Muscatel
Grassy   Flowery

💬 ADDITIONAL NOTES

_____
_____
_____
_____
_____
_____
_____
_____
_____
_____
_____

🧊 PREPARED WITH

☐ Milk   ☐ Lemon
☐ Sugar   ☐ Honey
☐ Cream   ☐

☆ SCORE

/5 ☆

TEA Tasting

NAME	
ORIGIN	METHOD
VENDOR	MEASURE
PRICE	STEEP TIME
TASTING DATE	TEMP

🫖 TEA TYPE

☐ White ☐ Green ☐ Oolong ☐ Black ☐ Pu-erh ☐ Herbal ☐

🌿 DRY LEAF

🌿 INFUSED LEAF

☕ LIQUOR

👁 LOOK

☐ Clear ☐ Semi-Cloudy ☐ Cloudy
_____
_____

👃 AROMA

☐ Low ☐ Med. ☐ High Complexity
_____
_____
_____
_____
_____

🫖 PALATE

☐ Bright ☐ Smooth ☐ Light
☐ Soft ☐ Medium ☐ Medium
☐ Dull ☐ Harsh ☐ Full-Bodied
_____
_____
_____
_____
_____
_____

👄 FINISH

☐ Short ☐ Medium ☐ Long
_____
_____
_____

😋 FLAVOR WHEEL

Earthy/Woodsy Smoky Nutty/Malty
Sweet
Sour Metallic
Fruity Milky
Spicy Bitter
Herbal Mineral
Vegetal Muscatel
Grassy Flowery

💬 ADDITIONAL NOTES

🧊 PREPARED WITH

☐ Milk ☐ Lemon
☐ Sugar ☐ Honey
☐ Cream ☐

☆ SCORE

/5 ☆

54

TEA Tasting

NAME	
ORIGIN	METHOD
VENDOR	MEASURE
PRICE	STEEP TIME
TASTING DATE	TEMP

🏷️ TEA TYPE

☐ White ☐ Green ☐ Oolong ☐ Black ☐ Pu-erh ☐ Herbal ☐

🌱 DRY LEAF
🌱 INFUSED LEAF

☕ LIQUOR

👁️ LOOK

☐ Clear ☐ Semi-Cloudy ☐ Cloudy
_____
_____

👃 AROMA

☐ Low ☐ Med. ☐ High Complexity
_____
_____
_____
_____

👅 PALATE

☐ Bright ☐ Smooth ☐ Light
☐ Soft ☐ Medium ☐ Medium
☐ Dull ☐ Harsh ☐ Full-Bodied
_____
_____
_____
_____
_____
_____
_____

👄 FINISH

☐ Short ☐ Medium ☐ Long
_____
_____
_____

😋 FLAVOR WHEEL

Earthy / Woodsy   Smoky   Nutty / Malty
Sweet
Sour   Metallic
Fruity   Milky
Spicy   Bitter
Herbal   Mineral
Vegetal   Muscatel
Grassy   Flowery

💬 ADDITIONAL NOTES

_____
_____
_____
_____
_____
_____
_____
_____
_____
_____
_____

🧊 PREPARED WITH

☐ Milk ☐ Lemon
☐ Sugar ☐ Honey
☐ Cream ☐

⭐ SCORE

/5 ☆

TEA Tasting

NAME	
ORIGIN	METHOD
VENDOR	MEASURE
PRICE	STEEP TIME
TASTING DATE	TEMP

🏷️ TEA TYPE

☐ White ☐ Green ☐ Oolong ☐ Black ☐ Pu-erh ☐ Herbal ☐

🌿 DRY LEAF | 🌱 INFUSED LEAF

☕ LIQUOR

👁 LOOK
☐ Clear ☐ Semi-Cloudy ☐ Cloudy

👃 AROMA
☐ Low ☐ Med. ☐ High Complexity

👅 PALATE
☐ Bright ☐ Smooth ☐ Light
☐ Soft ☐ Medium ☐ Medium
☐ Dull ☐ Harsh ☐ Full-Bodied

👄 FINISH
☐ Short ☐ Medium ☐ Long

😋 FLAVOR WHEEL

Earthy / Woodsy   Smoky   Nutty / Malty
Sweet
Sour   Metallic
Fruity   Milky
Spicy   Bitter
Herbal   Mineral
Vegetal   Muscatel
Grassy   Flowery

💬 ADDITIONAL NOTES

🧊 PREPARED WITH

☐ Milk ☐ Lemon
☐ Sugar ☐ Honey
☐ Cream ☐

☆ SCORE

/5 ☆

56

TEA Tasting

NAME		
ORIGIN	METHOD	
VENDOR	MEASURE	
PRICE	STEEP TIME	
TASTING DATE	TEMP	

🫖 TEA TYPE

☐ White ☐ Green ☐ Oolong ☐ Black ☐ Pu-erh ☐ Herbal ☐

🌿 DRY LEAF

🌱 INFUSED LEAF

☕ LIQUOR

LOOK
☐ Clear ☐ Semi-Cloudy ☐ Cloudy
_____
_____

AROMA
☐ Low ☐ Med. ☐ High Complexity
_____
_____
_____
_____

PALATE
☐ Bright ☐ Smooth ☐ Light
☐ Soft ☐ Medium ☐ Medium
☐ Dull ☐ Harsh ☐ Full-Bodied
_____
_____
_____
_____
_____
_____

FINISH
☐ Short ☐ Medium ☐ Long
_____
_____
_____

😋 FLAVOR WHEEL

Earthy / Woodsy — Smoky — Nutty / Malty
Sweet — Metallic
Sour — Milky
Fruity — Bitter
Spicy — Mineral
Herbal — Muscatel
Vegetal — Flowery
Grassy

💬 ADDITIONAL NOTES

🧊 PREPARED WITH

☐ Milk ☐ Lemon
☐ Sugar ☐ Honey
☐ Cream ☐

☆ SCORE

/5 ☆

TEA Tasting

NAME	
ORIGIN	METHOD
VENDOR	MEASURE
PRICE	STEEP TIME
TASTING DATE	TEMP

🔒 TEA TYPE

☐ White ☐ Green ☐ Oolong ☐ Black ☐ Pu-erh ☐ Herbal ☐

🌿 DRY LEAF / 🍃 INFUSED LEAF

☕ LIQUOR

LOOK
☐ Clear ☐ Semi-Cloudy ☐ Cloudy
_____
_____

AROMA
☐ Low ☐ Med. ☐ High Complexity
_____
_____
_____
_____

PALATE
☐ Bright ☐ Smooth ☐ Light
☐ Soft ☐ Medium ☐ Medium
☐ Dull ☐ Harsh ☐ Full-Bodied
_____
_____
_____
_____
_____
_____

FINISH
☐ Short ☐ Medium ☐ Long
_____
_____
_____

😋 FLAVOR WHEEL

Earthy/Woodsy Smoky Nutty/Malty
Sweet
Sour Metallic
Fruity Milky
Spicy Bitter
Herbal Mineral
Vegetal Muscatel
Grassy Flowery

💬 ADDITIONAL NOTES

🧊 PREPARED WITH

☐ Milk ☐ Lemon
☐ Sugar ☐ Honey
☐ Cream ☐

☆ SCORE

/5☆

TEA Tasting

NAME	
ORIGIN	METHOD
VENDOR	MEASURE
PRICE	STEEP TIME
TASTING DATE	TEMP

🔒 TEA TYPE

☐ White ☐ Green ☐ Oolong ☐ Black ☐ Pu-erh ☐ Herbal ☐

🌿 DRY LEAF

🌿 INFUSED LEAF

☕ LIQUOR

👁 LOOK

☐ Clear ☐ Semi-Cloudy ☐ Cloudy

👃 AROMA

☐ Low ☐ Med. ☐ High Complexity

👅 PALATE

☐ Bright ☐ Smooth ☐ Light
☐ Soft ☐ Medium ☐ Medium
☐ Dull ☐ Harsh ☐ Full-Bodied

👄 FINISH

☐ Short ☐ Medium ☐ Long

😋 FLAVOR WHEEL

Earthy / Woodsy Smoky Nutty / Malty
Sweet
Sour Metallic
Fruity Milky
Spicy Bitter
Herbal Mineral
Vegetal Muscatel
Grassy Flowery

💬 ADDITIONAL NOTES

🧊 PREPARED WITH

☐ Milk ☐ Lemon
☐ Sugar ☐ Honey
☐ Cream ☐

☆ SCORE

/5 ☆

TEA
Tasting

NAME

ORIGIN	METHOD
VENDOR	MEASURE
PRICE	STEEP TIME
TASTING DATE	TEMP

🍵 TEA TYPE

☐ White ☐ Green ☐ Oolong ☐ Black ☐ Pu-erh ☐ Herbal ☐

🌱 DRY LEAF

🌱 INFUSED LEAF

🍵 LIQUOR

LOOK 👁
☐ Clear ☐ Semi-Cloudy ☐ Cloudy

AROMA 👃
☐ Low ☐ Med. ☐ High Complexity

PALATE 🍵
☐ Bright ☐ Smooth ☐ Light
☐ Soft ☐ Medium ☐ Medium
☐ Dull ☐ Harsh ☐ Full-Bodied

FINISH 👄
☐ Short ☐ Medium ☐ Long

😋 FLAVOR WHEEL

Earthy / Woodsy
Sweet
Sour
Fruity
Spicy
Herbal
Vegetal
Grassy
Smoky
Nutty / Malty
Metallic
Milky
Bitter
Mineral
Muscatel
Flowery

💬 ADDITIONAL NOTES

🧋 PREPARED WITH

☐ Milk ☐ Lemon
☐ Sugar ☐ Honey
☐ Cream ☐

☆ SCORE

/5 ☆

60

TEA Tasting

NAME	
ORIGIN	METHOD
VENDOR	MEASURE
PRICE	STEEP TIME
TASTING DATE	TEMP

🫖 TEA TYPE

☐ White ☐ Green ☐ Oolong ☐ Black ☐ Pu-erh ☐ Herbal ☐

🌱 DRY LEAF

🌿 INFUSED LEAF

☕ LIQUOR

👁 LOOK
☐ Clear ☐ Semi-Cloudy ☐ Cloudy
_____
_____

👃 AROMA
☐ Low ☐ Med. ☐ High Complexity
_____
_____
_____
_____

🥤 PALATE
☐ Bright ☐ Smooth ☐ Light
☐ Soft ☐ Medium ☐ Medium
☐ Dull ☐ Harsh ☐ Full-Bodied
_____
_____
_____
_____
_____
_____
_____

👄 FINISH
☐ Short ☐ Medium ☐ Long
_____
_____
_____

😋 FLAVOR WHEEL

Earthy/Woodsy   Smoky   Nutty/Malty
Sweet
Sour   Metallic
Fruity   Milky
Spicy   Bitter
Herbal   Mineral
Vegetal   Muscatel
Grassy   Flowery

💬 ADDITIONAL NOTES

_____
_____
_____
_____
_____
_____
_____
_____
_____

🧊 PREPARED WITH

☐ Milk ☐ Lemon
☐ Sugar ☐ Honey
☐ Cream ☐

☆ SCORE

/5 ☆

61

TEA Tasting

NAME	
ORIGIN	METHOD
VENDOR	MEASURE
PRICE	STEEP TIME
TASTING DATE	TEMP

🫖 TEA TYPE

☐ White ☐ Green ☐ Oolong ☐ Black ☐ Pu-erh ☐ Herbal ☐

🌿 DRY LEAF

🌿 INFUSED LEAF

☕ LIQUOR

👁 LOOK
☐ Clear ☐ Semi-Cloudy ☐ Cloudy

👃 AROMA
☐ Low ☐ Med. ☐ High Complexity

👅 PALATE
☐ Bright ☐ Smooth ☐ Light
☐ Soft ☐ Medium ☐ Medium
☐ Dull ☐ Harsh ☐ Full-Bodied

👄 FINISH
☐ Short ☐ Medium ☐ Long

😋 FLAVOR WHEEL

Earthy / Woodsy Smoky Nutty / Malty
Sweet
Sour Metallic
Fruity Milky
Spicy Bitter
Herbal Mineral
Vegetal Muscatel
Grassy Flowery

💬 ADDITIONAL NOTES

🧊 PREPARED WITH

☐ Milk ☐ Lemon
☐ Sugar ☐ Honey
☐ Cream ☐

☆ SCORE

/5 ☆

TEA Tasting

NAME	
ORIGIN	METHOD
VENDOR	MEASURE
PRICE	STEEP TIME
TASTING DATE	TEMP

🔒 TEA TYPE

☐ White ☐ Green ☐ Oolong ☐ Black ☐ Pu-erh ☐ Herbal ☐

🌿 DRY LEAF

🌿 INFUSED LEAF

☕ LIQUOR

👁 LOOK

☐ Clear ☐ Semi-Cloudy ☐ Cloudy

_____

_____

👃 AROMA

☐ Low ☐ Med. ☐ High Complexity

_____
_____
_____
_____

🫖 PALATE

☐ Bright ☐ Smooth ☐ Light
☐ Soft ☐ Medium ☐ Medium
☐ Dull ☐ Harsh ☐ Full-Bodied

_____
_____
_____
_____
_____
_____

👄 FINISH

☐ Short ☐ Medium ☐ Long

_____
_____
_____

😊 FLAVOR WHEEL

Earthy / Woodsy
Smoky
Nutty / Malty
Sweet
Sour
Metallic
Fruity
Milky
Spicy
Bitter
Herbal
Mineral
Vegetal
Muscatel
Grassy
Flowery

💬 ADDITIONAL NOTES

_____
_____
_____
_____
_____
_____
_____
_____
_____
_____
_____

🍬 PREPARED WITH

☐ Milk ☐ Lemon
☐ Sugar ☐ Honey
☐ Cream ☐

⭐ SCORE

/5 ☆

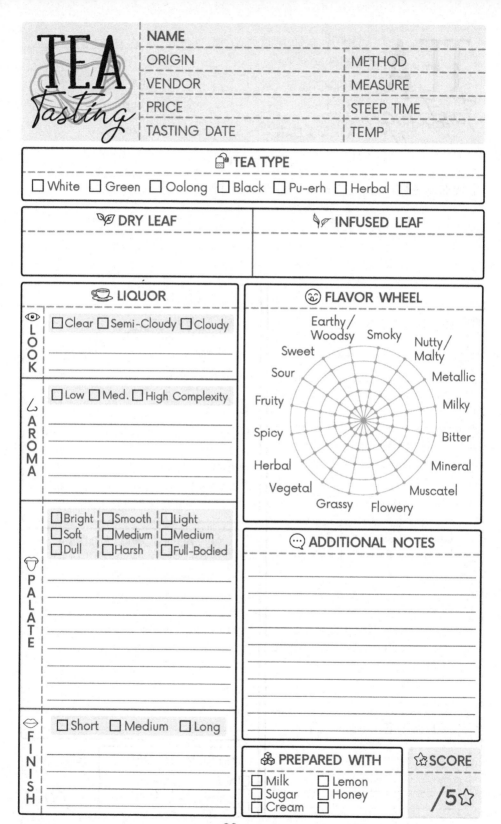

TEA Tasting

NAME	
ORIGIN	METHOD
VENDOR	MEASURE
PRICE	STEEP TIME
TASTING DATE	TEMP

🏷️ TEA TYPE

☐ White ☐ Green ☐ Oolong ☐ Black ☐ Pu-erh ☐ Herbal ☐

🌿 DRY LEAF

🌿 INFUSED LEAF

☕ LIQUOR

LOOK
☐ Clear ☐ Semi-Cloudy ☐ Cloudy
_____
_____

AROMA
☐ Low ☐ Med. ☐ High Complexity
_____
_____
_____
_____

PALATE
☐ Bright ☐ Smooth ☐ Light
☐ Soft ☐ Medium ☐ Medium
☐ Dull ☐ Harsh ☐ Full-Bodied
_____
_____
_____
_____
_____
_____

FINISH
☐ Short ☐ Medium ☐ Long
_____
_____
_____

😊 FLAVOR WHEEL

Earthy/Woodsy Smoky Nutty/Malty
Sweet
Sour   Metallic
Fruity   Milky
Spicy   Bitter
Herbal   Mineral
Vegetal   Muscatel
Grassy Flowery

💬 ADDITIONAL NOTES

_____
_____
_____
_____
_____
_____
_____
_____
_____

🧊 PREPARED WITH

☐ Milk ☐ Lemon
☐ Sugar ☐ Honey
☐ Cream ☐

⭐ SCORE

/5 ☆

TEA Tasting

NAME	
ORIGIN	METHOD
VENDOR	MEASURE
PRICE	STEEP TIME
TASTING DATE	TEMP

🔓 TEA TYPE

☐ White ☐ Green ☐ Oolong ☐ Black ☐ Pu-erh ☐ Herbal ☐

🌿 DRY LEAF	🌱 INFUSED LEAF

☕ LIQUOR

👁 LOOK
☐ Clear ☐ Semi-Cloudy ☐ Cloudy
_____
_____

👃 AROMA
☐ Low ☐ Med. ☐ High Complexity
_____
_____
_____
_____

🫖 PALATE
☐ Bright ☐ Smooth ☐ Light
☐ Soft ☐ Medium ☐ Medium
☐ Dull ☐ Harsh ☐ Full-Bodied
_____
_____
_____
_____
_____
_____

👄 FINISH
☐ Short ☐ Medium ☐ Long
_____
_____
_____

😋 FLAVOR WHEEL

Earthy / Woodsy
Smoky
Nutty / Malty
Sweet
Sour
Metallic
Fruity
Milky
Spicy
Bitter
Herbal
Mineral
Vegetal
Muscatel
Grassy
Flowery

💬 ADDITIONAL NOTES
_____
_____
_____
_____
_____
_____
_____
_____
_____

🧊 PREPARED WITH
☐ Milk ☐ Lemon
☐ Sugar ☐ Honey
☐ Cream ☐

☆ SCORE

/5 ☆

TEA Tasting

NAME	
ORIGIN	METHOD
VENDOR	MEASURE
PRICE	STEEP TIME
TASTING DATE	TEMP

🏷 TEA TYPE

☐ White ☐ Green ☐ Oolong ☐ Black ☐ Pu-erh ☐ Herbal ☐

🌿 DRY LEAF

🌿 INFUSED LEAF

☕ LIQUOR

👁 LOOK
☐ Clear ☐ Semi-Cloudy ☐ Cloudy
_____
_____

👃 AROMA
☐ Low ☐ Med. ☐ High Complexity
_____
_____
_____
_____
_____

👅 PALATE
☐ Bright ☐ Smooth ☐ Light
☐ Soft ☐ Medium ☐ Medium
☐ Dull ☐ Harsh ☐ Full-Bodied
_____
_____
_____
_____
_____
_____

👄 FINISH
☐ Short ☐ Medium ☐ Long
_____
_____
_____

😋 FLAVOR WHEEL

Earthy / Woodsy — Smoky — Nutty / Malty
Sweet — Metallic
Sour — Milky
Fruity — Bitter
Spicy — Mineral
Herbal — Muscatel
Vegetal — Flowery
Grassy

💬 ADDITIONAL NOTES

_____
_____
_____
_____
_____
_____
_____
_____
_____
_____
_____
_____

🧊 PREPARED WITH

☐ Milk ☐ Lemon
☐ Sugar ☐ Honey
☐ Cream ☐

☆ SCORE

/5 ☆

TEA Tasting

NAME	
ORIGIN	METHOD
VENDOR	MEASURE
PRICE	STEEP TIME
TASTING DATE	TEMP

🫖 TEA TYPE

☐ White ☐ Green ☐ Oolong ☐ Black ☐ Pu-erh ☐ Herbal ☐

🌿 DRY LEAF

🌿 INFUSED LEAF

☕ LIQUOR

👁 LOOK
☐ Clear ☐ Semi-Cloudy ☐ Cloudy
_____
_____

👃 AROMA
☐ Low ☐ Med. ☐ High Complexity
_____
_____
_____
_____

🍵 PALATE
☐ Bright ☐ Smooth ☐ Light
☐ Soft ☐ Medium ☐ Medium
☐ Dull ☐ Harsh ☐ Full-Bodied
_____
_____
_____
_____
_____

👄 FINISH
☐ Short ☐ Medium ☐ Long
_____
_____

😋 FLAVOR WHEEL

Earthy/Woodsy Smoky Nutty/Malty
Sweet
Sour Metallic
Fruity Milky
Spicy Bitter
Herbal Mineral
Vegetal Muscatel
Grassy Flowery

💬 ADDITIONAL NOTES

_____
_____
_____
_____
_____
_____
_____
_____
_____
_____
_____
_____
_____

🧊 PREPARED WITH
☐ Milk ☐ Lemon
☐ Sugar ☐ Honey
☐ Cream ☐

☆ SCORE
/5 ☆

TEA Tasting

NAME	
ORIGIN	METHOD
VENDOR	MEASURE
PRICE	STEEP TIME
TASTING DATE	TEMP

🔒 TEA TYPE

☐ White ☐ Green ☐ Oolong ☐ Black ☐ Pu-erh ☐ Herbal ☐

🌿 DRY LEAF

🌱 INFUSED LEAF

☕ LIQUOR

LOOK

☐ Clear ☐ Semi-Cloudy ☐ Cloudy

_____
_____

AROMA

☐ Low ☐ Med. ☐ High Complexity

_____
_____
_____
_____

PALATE

☐ Bright ☐ Smooth ☐ Light
☐ Soft   ☐ Medium ☐ Medium
☐ Dull   ☐ Harsh   ☐ Full-Bodied

_____
_____
_____
_____
_____
_____

FINISH

☐ Short ☐ Medium ☐ Long

_____
_____
_____

😋 FLAVOR WHEEL

Earthy / Woodsy — Smoky — Nutty / Malty
Sweet
Sour — Metallic
Fruity — Milky
Spicy — Bitter
Herbal — Mineral
Vegetal — Muscatel
Grassy — Flowery

💬 ADDITIONAL NOTES

_____
_____
_____
_____
_____
_____
_____
_____
_____
_____
_____
_____

🧊 PREPARED WITH

☐ Milk   ☐ Lemon
☐ Sugar ☐ Honey
☐ Cream ☐

⭐ SCORE

/5 ☆

68

TEA Tasting

NAME	
ORIGIN	METHOD
VENDOR	MEASURE
PRICE	STEEP TIME
TASTING DATE	TEMP

🔖 TEA TYPE

☐ White ☐ Green ☐ Oolong ☐ Black ☐ Pu-erh ☐ Herbal ☐

🌿 DRY LEAF	🌿 INFUSED LEAF

☕ LIQUOR

👁 LOOK

☐ Clear ☐ Semi-Cloudy ☐ Cloudy

_____
_____

👃 AROMA

☐ Low ☐ Med. ☐ High Complexity

_____
_____
_____
_____

👅 PALATE

☐ Bright ☐ Smooth ☐ Light
☐ Soft ☐ Medium ☐ Medium
☐ Dull ☐ Harsh ☐ Full-Bodied

_____
_____
_____
_____
_____

👄 FINISH

☐ Short ☐ Medium ☐ Long

_____
_____
_____

😊 FLAVOR WHEEL

Earthy/Woodsy
Smoky
Nutty/Malty
Sweet
Sour
Metallic
Fruity
Milky
Spicy
Bitter
Herbal
Mineral
Vegetal
Muscatel
Grassy
Flowery

💬 ADDITIONAL NOTES

_____
_____
_____
_____
_____
_____
_____
_____

🧊 PREPARED WITH

☐ Milk ☐ Lemon
☐ Sugar ☐ Honey
☐ Cream ☐

☆ SCORE

/5 ☆

TEA Tasting

NAME	
ORIGIN	METHOD
VENDOR	MEASURE
PRICE	STEEP TIME
TASTING DATE	TEMP

🏷️ TEA TYPE

☐ White ☐ Green ☐ Oolong ☐ Black ☐ Pu-erh ☐ Herbal ☐

🌿 DRY LEAF

🌿 INFUSED LEAF

☕ LIQUOR

👁️ LOOK
☐ Clear ☐ Semi-Cloudy ☐ Cloudy
_____
_____

👃 AROMA
☐ Low ☐ Med. ☐ High Complexity
_____
_____
_____

👅 PALATE
☐ Bright ☐ Smooth ☐ Light
☐ Soft ☐ Medium ☐ Medium
☐ Dull ☐ Harsh ☐ Full-Bodied
_____
_____
_____
_____
_____
_____

👄 FINISH
☐ Short ☐ Medium ☐ Long
_____
_____

😋 FLAVOR WHEEL

Earthy / Woodsy — Smoky — Nutty / Malty — Sweet — Sour — Metallic — Fruity — Milky — Spicy — Bitter — Herbal — Mineral — Vegetal — Muscatel — Grassy — Flowery

💬 ADDITIONAL NOTES

🎲 PREPARED WITH

☐ Milk ☐ Lemon
☐ Sugar ☐ Honey
☐ Cream ☐

☆ SCORE

/5 ☆

TEA Tasting

NAME	
ORIGIN	METHOD
VENDOR	MEASURE
PRICE	STEEP TIME
TASTING DATE	TEMP

🍵 TEA TYPE

☐ White ☐ Green ☐ Oolong ☐ Black ☐ Pu-erh ☐ Herbal ☐

🌿 DRY LEAF	🌱 INFUSED LEAF

☕ LIQUOR

LOOK
☐ Clear ☐ Semi-Cloudy ☐ Cloudy
_____
_____

AROMA
☐ Low ☐ Med. ☐ High Complexity
_____
_____
_____
_____

PALATE
☐ Bright ☐ Smooth ☐ Light
☐ Soft ☐ Medium ☐ Medium
☐ Dull ☐ Harsh ☐ Full-Bodied
_____
_____
_____
_____
_____
_____
_____

FINISH
☐ Short ☐ Medium ☐ Long
_____
_____
_____

😋 FLAVOR WHEEL

Earthy/Woodsy Smoky Nutty/Malty
Sweet
Sour Metallic
Fruity Milky
Spicy Bitter
Herbal Mineral
Vegetal Muscatel
Grassy Flowery

💬 ADDITIONAL NOTES

_____
_____
_____
_____
_____
_____
_____
_____
_____
_____
_____
_____
_____

🧊 PREPARED WITH

☐ Milk ☐ Lemon
☐ Sugar ☐ Honey
☐ Cream ☐

☆ SCORE

/5 ☆

TEA Tasting

NAME	
ORIGIN	METHOD
VENDOR	MEASURE
PRICE	STEEP TIME
TASTING DATE	TEMP

🏷️ TEA TYPE

☐ White ☐ Green ☐ Oolong ☐ Black ☐ Pu-erh ☐ Herbal ☐

🌿 DRY LEAF

🌱 INFUSED LEAF

☕ LIQUOR

LOOK 👁️
☐ Clear ☐ Semi-Cloudy ☐ Cloudy
_____
_____

AROMA 👃
☐ Low ☐ Med. ☐ High Complexity
_____
_____
_____
_____

PALATE 🥄
☐ Bright ☐ Smooth ☐ Light
☐ Soft ☐ Medium ☐ Medium
☐ Dull ☐ Harsh ☐ Full-Bodied
_____
_____
_____
_____
_____
_____

FINISH 👄
☐ Short ☐ Medium ☐ Long
_____
_____

😋 FLAVOR WHEEL

Earthy / Woodsy Smoky Nutty / Malty
Sweet
Sour Metallic
Fruity Milky
Spicy Bitter
Herbal Mineral
Vegetal Muscatel
Grassy Flowery

💬 ADDITIONAL NOTES

🎲 PREPARED WITH

☐ Milk ☐ Lemon
☐ Sugar ☐ Honey
☐ Cream ☐

⭐ SCORE

/5 ☆

72

TEA Tasting

NAME	
ORIGIN	METHOD
VENDOR	MEASURE
PRICE	STEEP TIME
TASTING DATE	TEMP

🏷 TEA TYPE

☐ White ☐ Green ☐ Oolong ☐ Black ☐ Pu-erh ☐ Herbal ☐

🌿 DRY LEAF

🌿 INFUSED LEAF

☕ LIQUOR

LOOK

☐ Clear ☐ Semi-Cloudy ☐ Cloudy

_____
_____

AROMA

☐ Low ☐ Med. ☐ High Complexity

_____
_____
_____
_____

PALATE

☐ Bright ☐ Smooth ☐ Light
☐ Soft ☐ Medium ☐ Medium
☐ Dull ☐ Harsh ☐ Full-Bodied

_____
_____
_____
_____
_____

FINISH

☐ Short ☐ Medium ☐ Long

_____
_____

😋 FLAVOR WHEEL

Earthy/Woodsy Smoky Nutty/Malty
Sweet Metallic
Sour
Fruity Milky
Spicy Bitter
Herbal Mineral
Vegetal Muscatel
Grassy Flowery

💬 ADDITIONAL NOTES

_____
_____
_____
_____
_____
_____
_____
_____
_____
_____
_____
_____

🎲 PREPARED WITH

☐ Milk ☐ Lemon
☐ Sugar ☐ Honey
☐ Cream ☐

☆ SCORE

/5 ☆

TEA Tasting

NAME		
ORIGIN	METHOD	
VENDOR	MEASURE	
PRICE	STEEP TIME	
TASTING DATE	TEMP	

🫖 TEA TYPE

☐ White ☐ Green ☐ Oolong ☐ Black ☐ Pu-erh ☐ Herbal ☐

🌿 DRY LEAF | 🌱 INFUSED LEAF

☕ LIQUOR

LOOK
☐ Clear ☐ Semi-Cloudy ☐ Cloudy
_____
_____

AROMA
☐ Low ☐ Med. ☐ High Complexity
_____
_____
_____
_____

PALATE
☐ Bright ☐ Smooth ☐ Light
☐ Soft ☐ Medium ☐ Medium
☐ Dull ☐ Harsh ☐ Full-Bodied
_____
_____
_____
_____
_____
_____

FINISH
☐ Short ☐ Medium ☐ Long
_____
_____
_____

😋 FLAVOR WHEEL

Earthy/Woodsy Smoky Nutty/Malty
Sweet
Sour
Fruity
Spicy
Herbal
Vegetal
Grassy Flowery Muscatel Mineral Bitter Milky Metallic

💬 ADDITIONAL NOTES

_____
_____
_____
_____
_____
_____
_____
_____
_____
_____

🎲 PREPARED WITH

☐ Milk ☐ Lemon
☐ Sugar ☐ Honey
☐ Cream ☐

☆ SCORE

/5 ☆

TEA Tasting

NAME	
ORIGIN	METHOD
VENDOR	MEASURE
PRICE	STEEP TIME
TASTING DATE	TEMP

🔖 TEA TYPE

☐ White ☐ Green ☐ Oolong ☐ Black ☐ Pu-erh ☐ Herbal ☐

🌱 DRY LEAF

🌿 INFUSED LEAF

☕ LIQUOR

👁 LOOK
☐ Clear ☐ Semi-Cloudy ☐ Cloudy

👃 AROMA
☐ Low ☐ Med. ☐ High Complexity

👅 PALATE
☐ Bright ☐ Smooth ☐ Light
☐ Soft ☐ Medium ☐ Medium
☐ Dull ☐ Harsh ☐ Full-Bodied

👄 FINISH
☐ Short ☐ Medium ☐ Long

😋 FLAVOR WHEEL

Earthy / Woodsy Smoky Nutty / Malty
Sweet Metallic
Sour Milky
Fruity Bitter
Spicy Mineral
Herbal Muscatel
Vegetal Flowery
Grassy

💬 ADDITIONAL NOTES

🧊 PREPARED WITH

☐ Milk ☐ Lemon
☐ Sugar ☐ Honey
☐ Cream ☐

☆ SCORE

/5 ☆

TEA Tasting

NAME	
ORIGIN	METHOD
VENDOR	MEASURE
PRICE	STEEP TIME
TASTING DATE	TEMP

🏷️ TEA TYPE

☐ White ☐ Green ☐ Oolong ☐ Black ☐ Pu-erh ☐ Herbal ☐

🌿 DRY LEAF	🌱 INFUSED LEAF

☕ LIQUOR

LOOK
☐ Clear ☐ Semi-Cloudy ☐ Cloudy
_____
_____

AROMA
☐ Low ☐ Med. ☐ High Complexity
_____
_____
_____
_____

PALATE
☐ Bright ☐ Smooth ☐ Light
☐ Soft   ☐ Medium ☐ Medium
☐ Dull   ☐ Harsh   ☐ Full-Bodied
_____
_____
_____
_____
_____

FINISH
☐ Short ☐ Medium ☐ Long
_____
_____
_____

😋 FLAVOR WHEEL

Earthy / Woodsy · Smoky · Nutty / Malty · Sweet · Metallic · Sour · Fruity · Milky · Spicy · Bitter · Herbal · Mineral · Vegetal · Muscatel · Grassy · Flowery

💬 ADDITIONAL NOTES

_____
_____
_____
_____
_____
_____
_____
_____
_____
_____

🧊 PREPARED WITH

☐ Milk   ☐ Lemon
☐ Sugar   ☐ Honey
☐ Cream   ☐

☆ SCORE

/5 ☆

TEA Tasting

NAME	
ORIGIN	METHOD
VENDOR	MEASURE
PRICE	STEEP TIME
TASTING DATE	TEMP

🔓 TEA TYPE

☐ White ☐ Green ☐ Oolong ☐ Black ☐ Pu-erh ☐ Herbal ☐

🌿 DRY LEAF

🌿 INFUSED LEAF

☕ LIQUOR

👁 LOOK

☐ Clear ☐ Semi-Cloudy ☐ Cloudy

👃 AROMA

☐ Low ☐ Med. ☐ High Complexity

👅 PALATE

☐ Bright ☐ Smooth ☐ Light
☐ Soft ☐ Medium ☐ Medium
☐ Dull ☐ Harsh ☐ Full-Bodied

👄 FINISH

☐ Short ☐ Medium ☐ Long

😋 FLAVOR WHEEL

Earthy/Woodsy Smoky Nutty/Malty
Sweet
Sour Metallic
Fruity Milky
Spicy Bitter
Herbal Mineral
Vegetal Muscatel
Grassy Flowery

💬 ADDITIONAL NOTES

🧊 PREPARED WITH

☐ Milk ☐ Lemon
☐ Sugar ☐ Honey
☐ Cream ☐

☆ SCORE

/5 ☆

TEA Tasting

NAME	
ORIGIN	METHOD
VENDOR	MEASURE
PRICE	STEEP TIME
TASTING DATE	TEMP

🍵 TEA TYPE

☐ White ☐ Green ☐ Oolong ☐ Black ☐ Pu-erh ☐ Herbal ☐

🌿 DRY LEAF

🌿 INFUSED LEAF

🍵 LIQUOR

👁 LOOK
☐ Clear ☐ Semi-Cloudy ☐ Cloudy

👃 AROMA
☐ Low ☐ Med. ☐ High Complexity

👅 PALATE
☐ Bright ☐ Smooth ☐ Light
☐ Soft ☐ Medium ☐ Medium
☐ Dull ☐ Harsh ☐ Full-Bodied

👄 FINISH
☐ Short ☐ Medium ☐ Long

😋 FLAVOR WHEEL

Earthy / Woodsy Smoky Nutty / Malty
Sweet
Sour Metallic
Fruity Milky
Spicy Bitter
Herbal Mineral
Vegetal Muscatel
Grassy Flowery

💬 ADDITIONAL NOTES

🎲 PREPARED WITH

☐ Milk ☐ Lemon
☐ Sugar ☐ Honey
☐ Cream ☐

☆ SCORE

/5 ☆

TEA Tasting

NAME	
ORIGIN	METHOD
VENDOR	MEASURE
PRICE	STEEP TIME
TASTING DATE	TEMP

🏷️ TEA TYPE

☐ White ☐ Green ☐ Oolong ☐ Black ☐ Pu-erh ☐ Herbal ☐

🌿 DRY LEAF

🌿 INFUSED LEAF

☕ LIQUOR

👁️ LOOK

☐ Clear ☐ Semi-Cloudy ☐ Cloudy

_____
_____

👃 AROMA

☐ Low ☐ Med. ☐ High Complexity

_____
_____
_____
_____

👅 PALATE

☐ Bright ☐ Smooth ☐ Light
☐ Soft ☐ Medium ☐ Medium
☐ Dull ☐ Harsh ☐ Full-Bodied

_____
_____
_____
_____
_____
_____
_____

👄 FINISH

☐ Short ☐ Medium ☐ Long

_____
_____
_____

😋 FLAVOR WHEEL

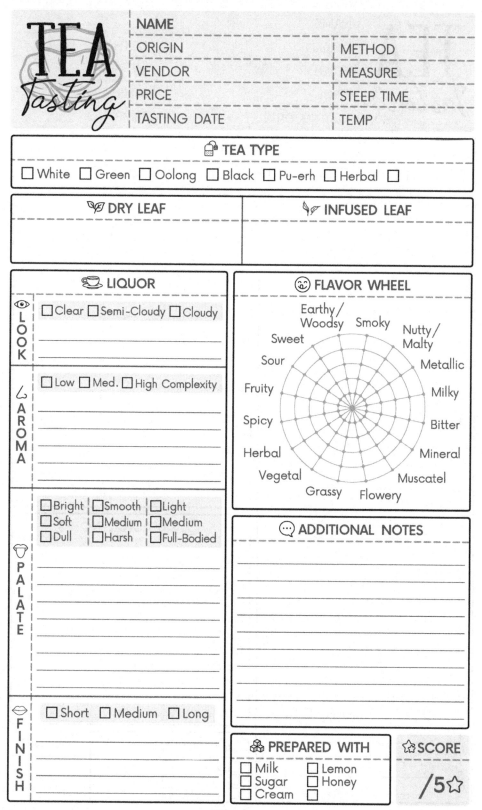

Earthy/Woodsy Smoky Nutty/Malty
Sweet
Sour Metallic
Fruity Milky
Spicy Bitter
Herbal Mineral
Vegetal Muscatel
Grassy Flowery

💬 ADDITIONAL NOTES

_____
_____
_____
_____
_____
_____
_____
_____
_____
_____
_____

🧊 PREPARED WITH

☐ Milk ☐ Lemon
☐ Sugar ☐ Honey
☐ Cream ☐

☆ SCORE

/5 ☆

TEA Tasting

NAME	
ORIGIN	METHOD
VENDOR	MEASURE
PRICE	STEEP TIME
TASTING DATE	TEMP

🫖 TEA TYPE

☐ White ☐ Green ☐ Oolong ☐ Black ☐ Pu-erh ☐ Herbal ☐

🌿 DRY LEAF | 🌱 INFUSED LEAF

☕ LIQUOR

👁 LOOK
☐ Clear ☐ Semi-Cloudy ☐ Cloudy

_____
_____

👃 AROMA
☐ Low ☐ Med. ☐ High Complexity

_____
_____
_____
_____

👅 PALATE
☐ Bright ☐ Smooth ☐ Light
☐ Soft   ☐ Medium ☐ Medium
☐ Dull   ☐ Harsh   ☐ Full-Bodied

_____
_____
_____
_____
_____
_____
_____

👄 FINISH
☐ Short ☐ Medium ☐ Long

_____
_____
_____

😋 FLAVOR WHEEL

Earthy/Woodsy Smoky Nutty/Malty
Sweet
Sour   Metallic
Fruity   Milky
Spicy   Bitter
Herbal   Mineral
Vegetal   Muscatel
Grassy Flowery

💬 ADDITIONAL NOTES

_____
_____
_____
_____
_____
_____
_____
_____
_____
_____
_____
_____

🧊 PREPARED WITH

☐ Milk   ☐ Lemon
☐ Sugar   ☐ Honey
☐ Cream   ☐

☆ SCORE

/5 ☆

TEA Tasting

NAME	
ORIGIN	METHOD
VENDOR	MEASURE
PRICE	STEEP TIME
TASTING DATE	TEMP

🔒 TEA TYPE

☐ White ☐ Green ☐ Oolong ☐ Black ☐ Pu-erh ☐ Herbal ☐

🌱 DRY LEAF

🍃 INFUSED LEAF

☕ LIQUOR

LOOK
☐ Clear ☐ Semi-Cloudy ☐ Cloudy
_____
_____

AROMA
☐ Low ☐ Med. ☐ High Complexity
_____
_____
_____
_____

PALATE
☐ Bright ☐ Smooth ☐ Light
☐ Soft ☐ Medium ☐ Medium
☐ Dull ☐ Harsh ☐ Full-Bodied
_____
_____
_____
_____
_____
_____

FINISH
☐ Short ☐ Medium ☐ Long
_____
_____
_____

😋 FLAVOR WHEEL

Earthy/Woodsy Smoky Nutty/Malty
Sweet Metallic
Sour
Fruity Milky
Spicy Bitter
Herbal Mineral
Vegetal Muscatel
Grassy Flowery

💬 ADDITIONAL NOTES

🍯 PREPARED WITH

☐ Milk ☐ Lemon
☐ Sugar ☐ Honey
☐ Cream ☐

☆ SCORE

/5 ☆

TEA Tasting

NAME	
ORIGIN	METHOD
VENDOR	MEASURE
PRICE	STEEP TIME
TASTING DATE	TEMP

🏷️ TEA TYPE

☐ White   ☐ Green   ☐ Oolong   ☐ Black   ☐ Pu-erh   ☐ Herbal   ☐

🌿 DRY LEAF | 🌱 INFUSED LEAF

☕ LIQUOR

👁️ LOOK
☐ Clear ☐ Semi-Cloudy ☐ Cloudy
_____
_____

👃 AROMA
☐ Low ☐ Med. ☐ High Complexity
_____
_____
_____

🫖 PALATE
☐ Bright   ☐ Smooth   ☐ Light
☐ Soft   ☐ Medium   ☐ Medium
☐ Dull   ☐ Harsh   ☐ Full-Bodied
_____
_____
_____
_____
_____

👄 FINISH
☐ Short ☐ Medium ☐ Long
_____
_____

😋 FLAVOR WHEEL

Earthy / Woodsy   Smoky   Nutty / Malty
Sweet
Sour   Metallic
Fruity   Milky
Spicy   Bitter
Herbal   Mineral
Vegetal   Muscatel
Grassy   Flowery

💬 ADDITIONAL NOTES

🧊 PREPARED WITH

☐ Milk   ☐ Lemon
☐ Sugar   ☐ Honey
☐ Cream   ☐

⭐ SCORE

/5 ☆

82

TEA Tasting

NAME	
ORIGIN	METHOD
VENDOR	MEASURE
PRICE	STEEP TIME
TASTING DATE	TEMP

🫖 TEA TYPE

☐ White ☐ Green ☐ Oolong ☐ Black ☐ Pu-erh ☐ Herbal ☐

🌿 DRY LEAF	🌱 INFUSED LEAF

☕ LIQUOR

👁 LOOK

☐ Clear ☐ Semi-Cloudy ☐ Cloudy

_____
_____

👃 AROMA

☐ Low ☐ Med. ☐ High Complexity

_____
_____
_____
_____

👅 PALATE

☐ Bright ☐ Smooth ☐ Light
☐ Soft ☐ Medium ☐ Medium
☐ Dull ☐ Harsh ☐ Full-Bodied

_____
_____
_____
_____
_____
_____

👄 FINISH

☐ Short ☐ Medium ☐ Long

_____
_____
_____

😋 FLAVOR WHEEL

Earthy/Woodsy Smoky Nutty/Malty
Sweet Metallic
Sour Milky
Fruity Bitter
Spicy Mineral
Herbal Muscatel
Vegetal Flowery
Grassy

💬 ADDITIONAL NOTES

_____
_____
_____
_____
_____
_____
_____
_____
_____
_____
_____
_____

🧊 PREPARED WITH

☐ Milk ☐ Lemon
☐ Sugar ☐ Honey
☐ Cream ☐

☆ SCORE

/5 ☆

TEA Tasting

NAME	
ORIGIN	METHOD
VENDOR	MEASURE
PRICE	STEEP TIME
TASTING DATE	TEMP

🫖 TEA TYPE

☐ White ☐ Green ☐ Oolong ☐ Black ☐ Pu-erh ☐ Herbal ☐

🌿 DRY LEAF

🌱 INFUSED LEAF

☕ LIQUOR

LOOK 👁
☐ Clear ☐ Semi-Cloudy ☐ Cloudy
_____
_____

AROMA 👃
☐ Low ☐ Med. ☐ High Complexity
_____
_____
_____
_____

PALATE 👅
☐ Bright ☐ Smooth ☐ Light
☐ Soft ☐ Medium ☐ Medium
☐ Dull ☐ Harsh ☐ Full-Bodied
_____
_____
_____
_____
_____

FINISH 👄
☐ Short ☐ Medium ☐ Long
_____
_____
_____

😋 FLAVOR WHEEL

Earthy/Woodsy Smoky Nutty/Malty
Sweet
Sour   Metallic
Fruity   Milky
Spicy   Bitter
Herbal   Mineral
Vegetal   Muscatel
Grassy Flowery

💬 ADDITIONAL NOTES

✿ PREPARED WITH

☐ Milk ☐ Lemon
☐ Sugar ☐ Honey
☐ Cream ☐

☆ SCORE

/5 ☆

TEA Tasting

NAME	
ORIGIN	METHOD
VENDOR	MEASURE
PRICE	STEEP TIME
TASTING DATE	TEMP

🫖 TEA TYPE

☐ White ☐ Green ☐ Oolong ☐ Black ☐ Pu-erh ☐ Herbal ☐

🌿 DRY LEAF

🌿 INFUSED LEAF

☕ LIQUOR

👁 LOOK

☐ Clear ☐ Semi-Cloudy ☐ Cloudy

_____
_____

👃 AROMA

☐ Low ☐ Med. ☐ High Complexity

_____
_____
_____
_____

🫖 PALATE

☐ Bright ☐ Smooth ☐ Light
☐ Soft ☐ Medium ☐ Medium
☐ Dull ☐ Harsh ☐ Full-Bodied

_____
_____
_____
_____
_____
_____

👄 FINISH

☐ Short ☐ Medium ☐ Long

_____
_____
_____

😋 FLAVOR WHEEL

Earthy/Woodsy   Smoky   Nutty/Malty
Sweet
Sour   Metallic
Fruity   Milky
Spicy   Bitter
Herbal   Mineral
Vegetal   Muscatel
Grassy   Flowery

💬 ADDITIONAL NOTES

_____
_____
_____
_____
_____
_____
_____
_____
_____
_____
_____

🎲 PREPARED WITH

☐ Milk ☐ Lemon
☐ Sugar ☐ Honey
☐ Cream ☐

☆ SCORE

/5 ☆

85

TEA Tasting

NAME	
ORIGIN	METHOD
VENDOR	MEASURE
PRICE	STEEP TIME
TASTING DATE	TEMP

🔒 TEA TYPE

☐ White ☐ Green ☐ Oolong ☐ Black ☐ Pu-erh ☐ Herbal ☐

🌱 DRY LEAF

🌱 INFUSED LEAF

☕ LIQUOR

👁 LOOK

☐ Clear ☐ Semi-Cloudy ☐ Cloudy

_____
_____

👃 AROMA

☐ Low ☐ Med. ☐ High Complexity

_____
_____
_____
_____

🍵 PALATE

☐ Bright ☐ Smooth ☐ Light
☐ Soft ☐ Medium ☐ Medium
☐ Dull ☐ Harsh ☐ Full-Bodied

_____
_____
_____
_____
_____

👄 FINISH

☐ Short ☐ Medium ☐ Long

_____
_____
_____

☺ FLAVOR WHEEL

Earthy / Woodsy Smoky Nutty / Malty
Sweet
Sour   Metallic
Fruity   Milky
Spicy   Bitter
Herbal   Mineral
Vegetal   Muscatel
Grassy Flowery

💬 ADDITIONAL NOTES

🎲 PREPARED WITH

☐ Milk   ☐ Lemon
☐ Sugar   ☐ Honey
☐ Cream   ☐

☆ SCORE

/5 ☆

86

TEA Tasting

NAME		
ORIGIN		METHOD
VENDOR		MEASURE
PRICE		STEEP TIME
TASTING DATE		TEMP

🏷️ TEA TYPE

☐ White ☐ Green ☐ Oolong ☐ Black ☐ Pu-erh ☐ Herbal ☐

🌱 DRY LEAF

🌿 INFUSED LEAF

☕ LIQUOR

👁️ LOOK

☐ Clear ☐ Semi-Cloudy ☐ Cloudy

_____

_____

👃 AROMA

☐ Low ☐ Med. ☐ High Complexity

_____

_____

_____

_____

🍵 PALATE

☐ Bright ☐ Smooth ☐ Light
☐ Soft ☐ Medium ☐ Medium
☐ Dull ☐ Harsh ☐ Full-Bodied

_____

_____

_____

_____

_____

_____

👄 FINISH

☐ Short ☐ Medium ☐ Long

_____

_____

_____

😋 FLAVOR WHEEL

Earthy/Woodsy   Smoky   Nutty/Malty
Sweet
Sour   Metallic
Fruity   Milky
Spicy   Bitter
Herbal   Mineral
Vegetal   Muscatel
Grassy   Flowery

💬 ADDITIONAL NOTES

_____

_____

_____

_____

_____

_____

_____

_____

_____

_____

🧊 PREPARED WITH

☐ Milk ☐ Lemon
☐ Sugar ☐ Honey
☐ Cream ☐

☆ SCORE

/5 ☆

TEA
Tasting

NAME	
ORIGIN	METHOD
VENDOR	MEASURE
PRICE	STEEP TIME
TASTING DATE	TEMP

🏷 TEA TYPE

☐ White ☐ Green ☐ Oolong ☐ Black ☐ Pu-erh ☐ Herbal ☐

🌿 DRY LEAF | 🌱 INFUSED LEAF

☕ LIQUOR

👁 LOOK
☐ Clear ☐ Semi-Cloudy ☐ Cloudy
_____
_____

👃 AROMA
☐ Low ☐ Med. ☐ High Complexity
_____
_____
_____
_____
_____

👅 PALATE
☐ Bright ☐ Smooth ☐ Light
☐ Soft ☐ Medium ☐ Medium
☐ Dull ☐ Harsh ☐ Full-Bodied
_____
_____
_____
_____
_____
_____

👄 FINISH
☐ Short ☐ Medium ☐ Long
_____
_____
_____

😋 FLAVOR WHEEL

Earthy/Woodsy · Smoky · Nutty/Malty
Sweet · Metallic
Sour · Milky
Fruity
Spicy · Bitter
Herbal · Mineral
Vegetal · Muscatel
Grassy · Flowery

💬 ADDITIONAL NOTES

_____
_____
_____
_____
_____
_____
_____
_____
_____
_____
_____

🧊 PREPARED WITH

☐ Milk ☐ Lemon
☐ Sugar ☐ Honey
☐ Cream ☐

☆ SCORE

/5 ☆

88

TEA Tasting

NAME	
ORIGIN	METHOD
VENDOR	MEASURE
PRICE	STEEP TIME
TASTING DATE	TEMP

🍵 TEA TYPE

☐ White ☐ Green ☐ Oolong ☐ Black ☐ Pu-erh ☐ Herbal ☐

🌿 DRY LEAF

🌿 INFUSED LEAF

☕ LIQUOR

👁 LOOK

☐ Clear ☐ Semi-Cloudy ☐ Cloudy

_____
_____

👃 AROMA

☐ Low ☐ Med. ☐ High Complexity

_____
_____
_____
_____

👅 PALATE

☐ Bright ☐ Smooth ☐ Light
☐ Soft ☐ Medium ☐ Medium
☐ Dull ☐ Harsh ☐ Full-Bodied

_____
_____
_____
_____
_____
_____

👄 FINISH

☐ Short ☐ Medium ☐ Long

_____
_____
_____

😋 FLAVOR WHEEL

Earthy/Woodsy · Smoky · Nutty/Malty
Sweet · Metallic
Sour · Milky
Fruity · Bitter
Spicy · Mineral
Herbal · Muscatel
Vegetal · Grassy · Flowery

💬 ADDITIONAL NOTES

_____
_____
_____
_____
_____
_____
_____
_____
_____
_____
_____

🧊 PREPARED WITH

☐ Milk ☐ Lemon
☐ Sugar ☐ Honey
☐ Cream ☐

☆ SCORE

/5 ☆

TEA Tasting

NAME	
ORIGIN	METHOD
VENDOR	MEASURE
PRICE	STEEP TIME
TASTING DATE	TEMP

🍵 TEA TYPE

☐ White ☐ Green ☐ Oolong ☐ Black ☐ Pu-erh ☐ Herbal ☐

🌿 DRY LEAF

🌱 INFUSED LEAF

☕ LIQUOR

👁 LOOK

☐ Clear ☐ Semi-Cloudy ☐ Cloudy

_____
_____

👃 AROMA

☐ Low ☐ Med. ☐ High Complexity

_____
_____
_____
_____
_____

👅 PALATE

☐ Bright ☐ Smooth ☐ Light
☐ Soft ☐ Medium ☐ Medium
☐ Dull ☐ Harsh ☐ Full-Bodied

_____
_____
_____
_____
_____
_____

👄 FINISH

☐ Short ☐ Medium ☐ Long

_____
_____
_____

😋 FLAVOR WHEEL

Earthy / Woodsy
Smoky
Nutty / Malty
Sweet
Sour
Metallic
Fruity
Milky
Spicy
Bitter
Herbal
Mineral
Vegetal
Muscatel
Grassy
Flowery

💬 ADDITIONAL NOTES

_____
_____
_____
_____
_____
_____
_____
_____
_____
_____
_____

🧊 PREPARED WITH

☐ Milk ☐ Lemon
☐ Sugar ☐ Honey
☐ Cream ☐

☆ SCORE

/5 ☆

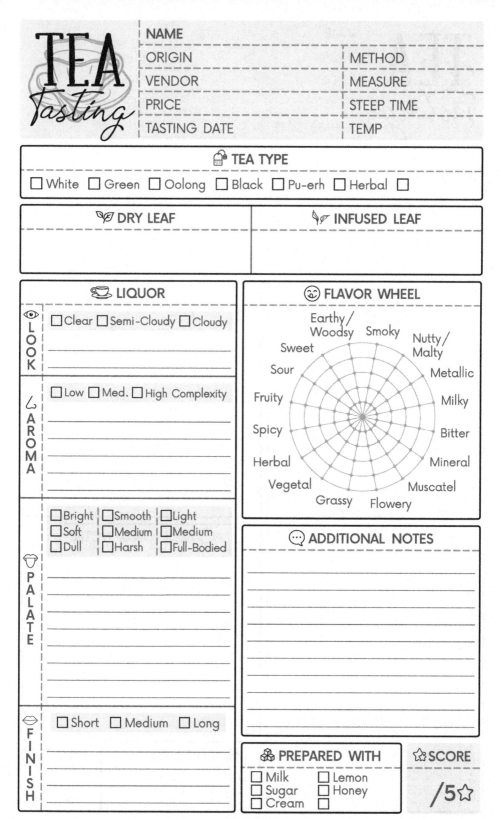

TEA Tasting

NAME	
ORIGIN	METHOD
VENDOR	MEASURE
PRICE	STEEP TIME
TASTING DATE	TEMP

🫖 TEA TYPE

☐ White ☐ Green ☐ Oolong ☐ Black ☐ Pu-erh ☐ Herbal ☐

🌿 DRY LEAF

🌱 INFUSED LEAF

☕ LIQUOR

👁 LOOK

☐ Clear ☐ Semi-Cloudy ☐ Cloudy

👃 AROMA

☐ Low ☐ Med. ☐ High Complexity

🍵 PALATE

☐ Bright ☐ Smooth ☐ Light
☐ Soft ☐ Medium ☐ Medium
☐ Dull ☐ Harsh ☐ Full-Bodied

👄 FINISH

☐ Short ☐ Medium ☐ Long

😋 FLAVOR WHEEL

Earthy/Woodsy Smoky Nutty/Malty
Sweet
Sour Metallic
Fruity Milky
Spicy Bitter
Herbal Mineral
Vegetal Muscatel
Grassy Flowery

💬 ADDITIONAL NOTES

🎲 PREPARED WITH

☐ Milk ☐ Lemon
☐ Sugar ☐ Honey
☐ Cream ☐

⭐ SCORE

/5 ☆

TEA
Tasting

NAME	
ORIGIN	METHOD
VENDOR	MEASURE
PRICE	STEEP TIME
TASTING DATE	TEMP

🫖 TEA TYPE

☐ White ☐ Green ☐ Oolong ☐ Black ☐ Pu-erh ☐ Herbal ☐

🌿 DRY LEAF

🌿 INFUSED LEAF

☕ LIQUOR

LOOK 👁
☐ Clear ☐ Semi-Cloudy ☐ Cloudy
_____
_____

AROMA 👃
☐ Low ☐ Med. ☐ High Complexity
_____
_____
_____
_____

PALATE 👅
☐ Bright ☐ Smooth ☐ Light
☐ Soft ☐ Medium ☐ Medium
☐ Dull ☐ Harsh ☐ Full-Bodied
_____
_____
_____
_____
_____
_____

FINISH 👄
☐ Short ☐ Medium ☐ Long
_____
_____
_____

😋 FLAVOR WHEEL

Earthy / Woodsy   Smoky   Nutty / Malty
Sweet
Sour   Metallic
Fruity   Milky
Spicy   Bitter
Herbal   Mineral
Vegetal   Muscatel
Grassy   Flowery

💬 ADDITIONAL NOTES

_____
_____
_____
_____
_____
_____
_____
_____
_____
_____
_____
_____
_____

🧊 PREPARED WITH

☐ Milk ☐ Lemon
☐ Sugar ☐ Honey
☐ Cream ☐

☆ SCORE

/5 ☆

TEA Tasting

NAME	
ORIGIN	METHOD
VENDOR	MEASURE
PRICE	STEEP TIME
TASTING DATE	TEMP

🍵 TEA TYPE

☐ White ☐ Green ☐ Oolong ☐ Black ☐ Pu-erh ☐ Herbal ☐

🌿 DRY LEAF	🌿 INFUSED LEAF

🍵 LIQUOR

👁 LOOK
☐ Clear ☐ Semi-Cloudy ☐ Cloudy

👃 AROMA
☐ Low ☐ Med. ☐ High Complexity

👅 PALATE
☐ Bright ☐ Smooth ☐ Light
☐ Soft ☐ Medium ☐ Medium
☐ Dull ☐ Harsh ☐ Full-Bodied

👄 FINISH
☐ Short ☐ Medium ☐ Long

😋 FLAVOR WHEEL

Earthy / Woodsy
Smoky
Nutty / Malty
Sweet
Metallic
Sour
Milky
Fruity
Spicy
Bitter
Herbal
Mineral
Vegetal
Muscatel
Grassy
Flowery

💬 ADDITIONAL NOTES

🧊 PREPARED WITH

☐ Milk ☐ Lemon
☐ Sugar ☐ Honey
☐ Cream ☐

☆ SCORE

/5 ☆

TEA Tasting

NAME	
ORIGIN	METHOD
VENDOR	MEASURE
PRICE	STEEP TIME
TASTING DATE	TEMP

🏷️ TEA TYPE

☐ White ☐ Green ☐ Oolong ☐ Black ☐ Pu-erh ☐ Herbal ☐

🍃 DRY LEAF

🍃 INFUSED LEAF

☕ LIQUOR

👁 LOOK

☐ Clear ☐ Semi-Cloudy ☐ Cloudy

_____
_____

👃 AROMA

☐ Low ☐ Med. ☐ High Complexity

_____
_____
_____
_____
_____

👅 PALATE

☐ Bright ☐ Smooth ☐ Light
☐ Soft ☐ Medium ☐ Medium
☐ Dull ☐ Harsh ☐ Full-Bodied

_____
_____
_____
_____
_____
_____

👄 FINISH

☐ Short ☐ Medium ☐ Long

_____
_____
_____

😋 FLAVOR WHEEL

Earthy / Woodsy   Smoky   Nutty / Malty
Sweet
Sour   Metallic
Fruity   Milky
Spicy   Bitter
Herbal   Mineral
Vegetal   Muscatel
Grassy   Flowery

💬 ADDITIONAL NOTES

_____
_____
_____
_____
_____
_____
_____
_____
_____
_____
_____
_____

🧊 PREPARED WITH

☐ Milk ☐ Lemon
☐ Sugar ☐ Honey
☐ Cream ☐

☆ SCORE

/5 ☆

94

TEA Tasting

NAME	
ORIGIN	METHOD
VENDOR	MEASURE
PRICE	STEEP TIME
TASTING DATE	TEMP

🍵 TEA TYPE

☐ White ☐ Green ☐ Oolong ☐ Black ☐ Pu-erh ☐ Herbal ☐

🌿 DRY LEAF	🌿 INFUSED LEAF

☕ LIQUOR

👁 LOOK

☐ Clear ☐ Semi-Cloudy ☐ Cloudy

_____

👃 AROMA

☐ Low ☐ Med. ☐ High Complexity

_____

👅 PALATE

☐ Bright ☐ Smooth ☐ Light
☐ Soft ☐ Medium ☐ Medium
☐ Dull ☐ Harsh ☐ Full-Bodied

_____

👄 FINISH

☐ Short ☐ Medium ☐ Long

😋 FLAVOR WHEEL

Earthy/Woodsy Smoky Nutty/Malty
Sweet
Sour Metallic
Fruity Milky
Spicy Bitter
Herbal Mineral
Vegetal Muscatel
Grassy Flowery

💬 ADDITIONAL NOTES

_____

🧊 PREPARED WITH

☐ Milk ☐ Lemon
☐ Sugar ☐ Honey
☐ Cream ☐

☆ SCORE

/5 ☆

TEA Tasting

NAME	
ORIGIN	METHOD
VENDOR	MEASURE
PRICE	STEEP TIME
TASTING DATE	TEMP

🏷️ TEA TYPE

☐ White ☐ Green ☐ Oolong ☐ Black ☐ Pu-erh ☐ Herbal ☐

🌿 DRY LEAF

🌱 INFUSED LEAF

☕ LIQUOR

LOOK
☐ Clear ☐ Semi-Cloudy ☐ Cloudy
_____
_____

AROMA
☐ Low ☐ Med. ☐ High Complexity
_____
_____
_____
_____

PALATE
☐ Bright ☐ Smooth ☐ Light
☐ Soft ☐ Medium ☐ Medium
☐ Dull ☐ Harsh ☐ Full-Bodied
_____
_____
_____
_____

FINISH
☐ Short ☐ Medium ☐ Long
_____
_____
_____

😋 FLAVOR WHEEL

Earthy / Woodsy Smoky Nutty / Malty
Sweet
Sour Metallic
Fruity Milky
Spicy Bitter
Herbal Mineral
Vegetal Muscatel
Grassy Flowery

💬 ADDITIONAL NOTES

_____
_____
_____
_____
_____
_____
_____
_____
_____

🧊 PREPARED WITH

☐ Milk ☐ Lemon
☐ Sugar ☐ Honey
☐ Cream ☐

☆ SCORE

/5 ☆

TEA Tasting

NAME	
ORIGIN	METHOD
VENDOR	MEASURE
PRICE	STEEP TIME
TASTING DATE	TEMP

🔖 TEA TYPE

☐ White ☐ Green ☐ Oolong ☐ Black ☐ Pu-erh ☐ Herbal ☐

🌱 DRY LEAF

🌿 INFUSED LEAF

☕ LIQUOR

👁 LOOK

☐ Clear ☐ Semi-Cloudy ☐ Cloudy
_____
_____

👃 AROMA

☐ Low ☐ Med. ☐ High Complexity
_____
_____
_____
_____

👅 PALATE

☐ Bright ☐ Smooth ☐ Light
☐ Soft ☐ Medium ☐ Medium
☐ Dull ☐ Harsh ☐ Full-Bodied
_____
_____
_____
_____
_____

👄 FINISH

☐ Short ☐ Medium ☐ Long
_____
_____
_____

😋 FLAVOR WHEEL

Earthy / Woodsy Smoky Nutty / Malty
Sweet
Sour Metallic
Fruity Milky
Spicy Bitter
Herbal Mineral
Vegetal Muscatel
Grassy Flowery

💬 ADDITIONAL NOTES

_____
_____
_____
_____
_____
_____
_____
_____
_____

🧉 PREPARED WITH

☐ Milk ☐ Lemon
☐ Sugar ☐ Honey
☐ Cream ☐

⭐ SCORE

/5 ☆

TEA Tasting

NAME	
ORIGIN	METHOD
VENDOR	MEASURE
PRICE	STEEP TIME
TASTING DATE	TEMP

🍵 TEA TYPE

☐ White ☐ Green ☐ Oolong ☐ Black ☐ Pu-erh ☐ Herbal ☐

🌿 DRY LEAF

🌱 INFUSED LEAF

🍵 LIQUOR

👁 LOOK
☐ Clear ☐ Semi-Cloudy ☐ Cloudy

👃 AROMA
☐ Low ☐ Med. ☐ High Complexity

👅 PALATE
☐ Bright ☐ Smooth ☐ Light
☐ Soft ☐ Medium ☐ Medium
☐ Dull ☐ Harsh ☐ Full-Bodied

👄 FINISH
☐ Short ☐ Medium ☐ Long

😋 FLAVOR WHEEL

Earthy / Woodsy · Smoky · Nutty / Malty · Sweet · Sour · Metallic · Fruity · Milky · Spicy · Bitter · Herbal · Mineral · Vegetal · Muscatel · Grassy · Flowery

💬 ADDITIONAL NOTES

🎲 PREPARED WITH

☐ Milk ☐ Lemon
☐ Sugar ☐ Honey
☐ Cream ☐

☆ SCORE

/5 ☆

98

TEA Tasting

NAME	
ORIGIN	METHOD
VENDOR	MEASURE
PRICE	STEEP TIME
TASTING DATE	TEMP

🔒 TEA TYPE

☐ White ☐ Green ☐ Oolong ☐ Black ☐ Pu-erh ☐ Herbal ☐

🌱 DRY LEAF	🌱 INFUSED LEAF

☕ LIQUOR

👁 LOOK
☐ Clear ☐ Semi-Cloudy ☐ Cloudy
_____
_____

👃 AROMA
☐ Low ☐ Med. ☐ High Complexity
_____
_____
_____
_____

👅 PALATE
☐ Bright ☐ Smooth ☐ Light
☐ Soft ☐ Medium ☐ Medium
☐ Dull ☐ Harsh ☐ Full-Bodied
_____
_____
_____
_____
_____

👄 FINISH
☐ Short ☐ Medium ☐ Long
_____
_____

😋 FLAVOR WHEEL

Earthy / Woodsy — Smoky — Nutty / Malty — Metallic — Milky — Bitter — Mineral — Muscatel — Flowery — Grassy — Vegetal — Herbal — Spicy — Fruity — Sour — Sweet

💬 ADDITIONAL NOTES

_____
_____
_____
_____
_____
_____
_____
_____
_____

🧊 PREPARED WITH

☐ Milk ☐ Lemon
☐ Sugar ☐ Honey
☐ Cream ☐

☆ SCORE

/5☆

TEA Tasting

NAME	
ORIGIN	METHOD
VENDOR	MEASURE
PRICE	STEEP TIME
TASTING DATE	TEMP

🔖 TEA TYPE

☐ White ☐ Green ☐ Oolong ☐ Black ☐ Pu-erh ☐ Herbal ☐

🌿 DRY LEAF

🍃 INFUSED LEAF

☕ LIQUOR

👁 LOOK

☐ Clear ☐ Semi-Cloudy ☐ Cloudy

_____
_____

👃 AROMA

☐ Low ☐ Med. ☐ High Complexity

_____
_____
_____
_____
_____

👅 PALATE

☐ Bright ☐ Smooth ☐ Light
☐ Soft ☐ Medium ☐ Medium
☐ Dull ☐ Harsh ☐ Full-Bodied

_____
_____
_____
_____
_____
_____

👄 FINISH

☐ Short ☐ Medium ☐ Long

_____
_____
_____

😋 FLAVOR WHEEL

Earthy/Woodsy · Smoky · Nutty/Malty · Sweet · Sour · Metallic · Fruity · Milky · Spicy · Bitter · Herbal · Mineral · Vegetal · Muscatel · Grassy · Flowery

💬 ADDITIONAL NOTES

_____
_____
_____
_____
_____
_____
_____
_____
_____
_____

🍬 PREPARED WITH

☐ Milk ☐ Lemon
☐ Sugar ☐ Honey
☐ Cream ☐

☆ SCORE

/5 ☆

TEA Tasting

NAME	
ORIGIN	METHOD
VENDOR	MEASURE
PRICE	STEEP TIME
TASTING DATE	TEMP

🍵 TEA TYPE

☐ White ☐ Green ☐ Oolong ☐ Black ☐ Pu-erh ☐ Herbal ☐

🌿 DRY LEAF

🌱 INFUSED LEAF

☕ LIQUOR

LOOK
☐ Clear ☐ Semi-Cloudy ☐ Cloudy
_____
_____

AROMA
☐ Low ☐ Med. ☐ High Complexity
_____
_____
_____
_____

PALATE
☐ Bright ☐ Smooth ☐ Light
☐ Soft ☐ Medium ☐ Medium
☐ Dull ☐ Harsh ☐ Full-Bodied
_____
_____
_____
_____
_____
_____

FINISH
☐ Short ☐ Medium ☐ Long
_____
_____
_____

😋 FLAVOR WHEEL

Earthy/Woodsy Smoky Nutty/Malty
Sweet Metallic
Sour
Fruity Milky
Spicy Bitter
Herbal Mineral
Vegetal Muscatel
Grassy Flowery

💬 ADDITIONAL NOTES

_____
_____
_____
_____
_____
_____
_____
_____
_____
_____
_____

🍬 PREPARED WITH

☐ Milk ☐ Lemon
☐ Sugar ☐ Honey
☐ Cream ☐

☆ SCORE

/5 ☆

TEA Tasting

NAME	
ORIGIN	METHOD
VENDOR	MEASURE
PRICE	STEEP TIME
TASTING DATE	TEMP

🫖 TEA TYPE

☐ White ☐ Green ☐ Oolong ☐ Black ☐ Pu-erh ☐ Herbal ☐

🌿 DRY LEAF

🌱 INFUSED LEAF

☕ LIQUOR

👁 LOOK

☐ Clear ☐ Semi-Cloudy ☐ Cloudy
_____
_____

👃 AROMA

☐ Low ☐ Med. ☐ High Complexity
_____
_____
_____
_____
_____

🫖 PALATE

☐ Bright ☐ Smooth ☐ Light
☐ Soft ☐ Medium ☐ Medium
☐ Dull ☐ Harsh ☐ Full-Bodied
_____
_____
_____
_____
_____
_____

👄 FINISH

☐ Short ☐ Medium ☐ Long
_____
_____
_____

😋 FLAVOR WHEEL

Earthy/Woodsy Smoky Nutty/Malty
Sweet
Sour   Metallic
Fruity   Milky
Spicy   Bitter
Herbal   Mineral
Vegetal   Muscatel
Grassy Flowery

💬 ADDITIONAL NOTES

_____
_____
_____
_____
_____
_____
_____
_____
_____
_____
_____
_____

🧊 PREPARED WITH

☐ Milk ☐ Lemon
☐ Sugar ☐ Honey
☐ Cream ☐

☆ SCORE

/5 ☆

TEA Tasting

NAME	
ORIGIN	METHOD
VENDOR	MEASURE
PRICE	STEEP TIME
TASTING DATE	TEMP

🔖 TEA TYPE

☐ White ☐ Green ☐ Oolong ☐ Black ☐ Pu-erh ☐ Herbal ☐

🌿 DRY LEAF	🌱 INFUSED LEAF

☕ LIQUOR

👁 **LOOK**

☐ Clear ☐ Semi-Cloudy ☐ Cloudy

_____
_____

👃 **AROMA**

☐ Low ☐ Med. ☐ High Complexity

_____
_____
_____
_____

👅 **PALATE**

☐ Bright ☐ Smooth ☐ Light
☐ Soft ☐ Medium ☐ Medium
☐ Dull ☐ Harsh ☐ Full-Bodied

_____
_____
_____
_____
_____
_____

👄 **FINISH**

☐ Short ☐ Medium ☐ Long

_____
_____
_____

😋 FLAVOR WHEEL

Earthy / Woodsy — Smoky — Nutty / Malty — Metallic — Milky — Bitter — Mineral — Muscatel — Flowery — Grassy — Vegetal — Herbal — Spicy — Fruity — Sour — Sweet

💬 ADDITIONAL NOTES

_____
_____
_____
_____
_____
_____
_____
_____
_____
_____

🍬 PREPARED WITH

☐ Milk ☐ Lemon
☐ Sugar ☐ Honey
☐ Cream ☐

☆ SCORE

/5 ☆

TEA Tasting

NAME	
ORIGIN	METHOD
VENDOR	MEASURE
PRICE	STEEP TIME
TASTING DATE	TEMP

🔒 TEA TYPE

☐ White ☐ Green ☐ Oolong ☐ Black ☐ Pu-erh ☐ Herbal ☐

🌿 DRY LEAF

🌱 INFUSED LEAF

☕ LIQUOR

👁 LOOK
☐ Clear ☐ Semi-Cloudy ☐ Cloudy
_____
_____

👃 AROMA
☐ Low ☐ Med. ☐ High Complexity
_____
_____
_____
_____

👅 PALATE
☐ Bright ☐ Smooth ☐ Light
☐ Soft ☐ Medium ☐ Medium
☐ Dull ☐ Harsh ☐ Full-Bodied
_____
_____
_____
_____
_____
_____

👄 FINISH
☐ Short ☐ Medium ☐ Long
_____
_____
_____

☺ FLAVOR WHEEL

Earthy/Woodsy Smoky Nutty/Malty
Sweet
Sour Metallic
Fruity Milky
Spicy Bitter
Herbal Mineral
Vegetal Muscatel
Grassy Flowery

💬 ADDITIONAL NOTES

_____
_____
_____
_____
_____
_____
_____
_____
_____

🍧 PREPARED WITH

☐ Milk ☐ Lemon
☐ Sugar ☐ Honey
☐ Cream ☐

☆ SCORE

/5☆

Made in United States
Orlando, FL
07 December 2024

55147215R00065